PAUL J. MEYER

AND THE
ART OF GIVING

JOHN EDMUND HAGGAI

KOBREY PRESS
Atlanta, Georgia

PAUL J. MEYER AND THE ART OF GIVING

ISBN 1-883108-04-7

For information, write
Dr. John Edmund Haggai
Haggai Institute
Post Office Box 13
Atlanta, Georgia 30370
U.S.A.

Printed by BAC Printers
Singapore

To those spiritual stalwarts

who, having heard God's truth

about the stewardship of money

at Haggai Institute,

have gone back to their respective nations

and led their people into the

joy of giving.

Blessed are the "doers of the Word
and not the hearers only" (James 1:22).

ACKNOWLEDGMENTS

My deep gratitude to —

Dr. Paul J. Meyer for dozens of hours spent in digging out documentary materials and candidly answering pertinent (some might even think, impertinent) questions.

Dr. William M. (Bill) Hinson, Paul's former pastor, friend, and colleague for nearly 40 years. Probably no man knows him like this remarkable confidant.

Mrs. Linda Peterson, Paul's executive secretary, for supplying more than 600 pages of information I needed for background research.

Mrs. Gladys W. Hudson, Paul's official biographer, for her personal insights and professional assistance.

Mr. David J. Lee of Scotland whose creativity, clarity of thought, writing and editing skills brought this oft-interrupted project to completion.

Miss Norma Byrd, my literary assistant, whose penchant for precision and proficiency in detail improved the text.

Mr. John Bachman, my personal assistant, who critiqued and proofread the manuscript.

And to Paul's many family members — especially his wife Jane — co-workers, friends, students, and even that rare detractor who contributed to this challenging undertaking.

CONTENTS

PREFACE

WHY I WROTE THIS BOOK

F or more than a decade I've said, "If I were to be asked to name my five most unforgettable characters, Paul J. Meyer would be in the group."

Since age 17, I have studied the lives of achievers and leaders. It's my view that not every achiever is a leader. But every leader is an achiever. Paul J. Meyer qualifies as a leader nonpareil. He's more than a producer; he's a creative life enhancer. He makes life easier and more meaningful for thousands of people on all continents.

Ask yourself: if a foreigner (say, an American) were to be stripped of all possessions and dropped off in some part of the world (say, Asia) where he knew no one, would he survive? Especially if he did not know the language? I believe Paul J. Meyer is one of those who would survive. More than that, in a short time he would thrive.

What's different about this man? Like all of us, he is a sinner. Thank God, he's a sinner saved by grace and walking with God. That's no different than the biography of millions of men. What impelled me to write this book?

Paul has worked since age eight. So have others. He grew up in poverty. So did others, including thousands of depression babies. (By depression I refer to the Great Depression that began that bleak October day in 1929.) His father treated him harshly. So have thousands of other fathers, especially those who brought "old country" habits to the United States. He decided against spending time in college. He opted, instead, to get the curriculum and books and study on his own. Others have done the same. He made millions. Others have also made millions.

So why has this man captured my interest and impelled me to write this book? Probably because he implements what he asserts to be his values and goals on a sustained basis. In his later sixties, he's still dreaming, planning, climbing, achieving. Every year

Paul addressing the annual meeting of his Waco employees. He treats his yardman and maid with the same respect he treats the President of the United States.

makes obsolete the previous year. He sets records, then breaks the records.

He sees possibilities and potentialities the average person never sees. Thirty years ago, with limited funds, he flew to Hong Kong. He knew nobody; he had the name of a man who had ordered an SMI (Success Motivation Institute) course. Within days, Paul saw the potential of moving into the multinational business arena. Today he operates in more than 60 nations. On his client roster, you find such names as the Union Bank of Switzerland, Daimler Benz, the German military, Coca Cola, Holiday Inn, General Electric, and Greyhound, plus major companies of that magnitude on every continent.

On a grander scale, and in every area of his life, he reminds me of my great Australian friend, the late Sir Hubert Opperman. In 1924, "Hubie" Opperman, a world-class cyclist, won the Tour de France. It was the first time a non-European won that contest. No one broke the record for 21 years. It was finally broken in 1945. Who broke it? None other than Hubert Opperman! That's Paul J. Meyer.

The public sees him bold as a lion, but they don't see the man who, in hours of thoughtful solitude, reads several books and listens to 20 cassettes a month. His admirers know he flies the world in a private jet; they don't see him alone flying his Piper Cub for hours. Many see him as a handsome gray-haired, well-built grandfather. They don't see him as a determined-to-win athlete who during the year involves himself in 23 different sports. Executives hardly turn their heads when they see him drive up in one of his luxury automobiles; they would suffer a neck-jerk to see him driving his 54-year-old pick-up truck.

He travels with no entourage; only with his wife Jane, family members, and special friends. He drives his own car. While he may entertain at a posh restaurant, he can also be seen with colleague Bill Hinson sitting on a bench outside eating a fat-free fruit yogurt for lunch. He treats his yardman and maid with the same respect he treats the president of the United States. He doesn't have one voice for one and another voice for the other. He neither postures nor preens. He's "real people."

He sits on only two boards; he detests board involvement. Despite the fact he has made millions through his skills as a communicator, he usually sits through two days of board meetings without saying a word. On those rare occasions when he does speak, everybody listens.

I've often said, "In my view, Paul overcommits and then keeps his commitments." He plans his time five years ahead and his giving three years ahead. Yet, a cry of need will find him ruthlessly wrenching his schedule to help. He spent half a day writing in detail his recommendations to a Mexican business executive who faced catastrophe. Paul's letter centered upon the importance of a Christ-centered life and letting God be in control.

Creative and productive people of Paul's caliber inevitably pay a price. The insecure and ambitious envy them. Their jealousy drives them to mockery, derision, defamation, and downright lying. As Rochefoucauld wrote years ago, "The jealous man poisons his own banquet, and then eats it." And Shakespeare wrote, "Oh, beware of jealousy; it is the green-eyed monster, which doth mock the meat it feeds on." No pleasure attaches to jealousy. It never enriches the jealous one. It shortens life and lessens health. It slays itself by its own knife. It shoots at others but wounds itself. It's stupid, costly, and nonproductive.

Paul moves ahead at such speed that I doubt he hears the criticisms occasionally leveled at him. If he did, he would not contaminate himself by contemplating the garbage dump from which it spreads. He invests his time only in what he calls "high pay off" activities.

And why waste time on what is demonstrably a fabrication? Over the years I've heard a few men question Paul's financial stability — "It's smoke and mirrors," one smirked. Well, you just may possibly live and give on Paul Meyer's scale by clever, high-leveraged, and grossly speculative borrowing. But you won't last long. Paul, however, has lived and performed at this level for nearly 40 years. And that's without family (or in-law) largesse, government grants, or winning the lottery.

Not only that. He's generous to his detractors. The Bible says a man's ox will fall in the very ditch he has dug for his neighbor's ox. I've seen that occur in Paul's experience. And then, amazingly, he turns around and helps his antagonist recover.

I like and believe the adage: "What Peter says about Paul tells more about Peter than it does about Paul."

When Paul turned 60, he set up his Passport to Success Program with a $5-million commitment. He quietly told of his prayer that during this decade of his life he would earn more and give more than he had during the first 60 years combined. He's on track.

Pygmy-minded, jealous critics can't handle that. Paul has enough money to maintain his current lifestyle the rest of his days. He could live a life of luxury — if he wanted to — and take it easy. But that's not for Paul. He possesses a God-given conviction, an inner drive to produce — to change the world. To that end, he continues to create, to multiply his resources, to inspire others to achieve.

The jealous critics will no more divert or decimate Paul's worldwide empire than the baying hound dog could stop Japan's fabulous bullet train. If only Paul's jealous detractors understood their self-destructive attitude, and Paul's eagerness to share what he knows, how greatly they would benefit.

A few months before writing these words, I read an article in a Texas publication about some Texas philanthropists. I applauded their generosity. However, in reality, Paul Meyer gives more every quarter than most of those men gave in a year, and Paul gives year after year after year. Once he gives, the beneficiary can know he will continue his interest, and they can set their calendar by the timing. He considers it cruel to give only once and spasmodically; the beneficiary suffers.

You may wonder why, with the exception of the book's subject, Paul J. Meyer, most of the philanthropists I mention are deceased. Simply this. I have not been privy to the financial information nor had opportunity to research thoroughly other living philanthropists. (A delightful exception is Henry D. Bronson of Chicago. He fits the designation "world-class engineer." I hope someday his story will be told.) Believe me, it's not a task you hurry. Years ago I wrote an article about a person well-known and respected across America. Alas, shortly thereafter, this person proved himself unworthy of respect, let alone of admiration. I decided then and there to guard carefully against a repeat of that embarrassment both to me and the person's family.

Paul founded Success Motivation Institute. When I first heard about it nearly 35 years ago, I wondered, "Is he a true success? Is he tied to the permanent?" It's my profound conviction that the only measure of worth — and of success — is permanence: how long it lasts.

Success means continuously and incrementally implementing God's will for your life. This obviates trampling on the rights of others — so often associated, in the minds of some, with success. More than that, it is my belief that true success depends on the art of giving, on the ability to give personally and financially through philanthropy. (The word "philanthropy" comes from two Greek words meaning "love of mankind.") In his skill and commitment in giving Paul Meyer has no parallel. That is no accident. His philanthropy and his success are inextricably linked.

By telling you about Paul Meyer, I want to show you why — and how — giving and success go together. So that you, too, can give freely, and you, too, can enjoy the fruits of true, deep, and lasting success. Success to you.

1

THE MAN WHO GAVE
EVERYTHING FOR NOTHING

Paul Meyer was heading for the biggest shock of his life. He pulled his white Cadillac into the lot behind National Union Life Insurance on 22nd and 8th, lifted a new leather attache case from the passenger seat, and climbed out. It was 7:30 a.m., a clear spring morning in Miami.

Paul Meyer was America's top sales agent. In his mid-twenties, he already had an entire agency under his control and more money than most men earn in a lifetime. But success hadn't left him complacent. Work to Paul Meyer was a discipline, and discipline began with the simple expedient of arriving before his staff. He paused only to brush a little dust off the Cadillac's hood before stepping briskly up to the one-time auto dealership that was National Union's home office in Florida. He turned the key, pushed the door open, entered.

Then he stopped dead.

The place was empty. Furniture, typewriters, filing cabinets, wastepaper baskets: everything had vanished. Save for one solitary potted plant, Paul had an unobstructed view across the old showroom to the plate glass windows and the 8th Avenue parking area. Even the carpet was gone.

He swallowed, lowered his attache case onto the bare floor, and wiped his hands together. They felt damp and prickly.

Gingerly — as though the place might be booby-trapped — he crossed the scuffed rectangular mark where the reception desk had been and swung open the door to the administration area. The same. A wall calendar remained. A black phone on a bundle of flex. Scattered papers. Apart from that, nothing. It was like landing in a science-fiction movie. Martians overrunning the planet. Was he in the right building?

Returning to the showroom he heard voices outside. They burst in, faltered, and fell silent. Bill Armor and Sonny Matisse.

Armor was Paul's closest friend and colleague; Matisse, a tall man with wispy gray hair, the company's most experienced salesman, an astute closer. Matisse threw a slack-jawed glance over his shoulder, as though the last box of files were being carted out to the lot.

Paul said, "What's going on?"

"You moving the office?"

"I just arrived here."

"Has there been a break-in, or what?"

"Come on, Sonny. Who in his right mind would take the carpet? Even the phone books are gone, for goodness sake."

"This is crazy," said Armor.

There was a pause, then Paul said, "Well, I guess we phone Basil."

Basil Autrey was National Union's founder and managing director.

Other people were turning up now. Junior sales staff, some of the secretaries. They looked around, dumbstruck. Fending off questions, Paul pushed his way into the administration area and scooped the phone up off the floor. He had to hold the base in one hand and the receiver in the other. Basil's number rang. And rang.

Bill Armor's eye caught Paul's.

"Nothing?"

Paul shook his head, clicked the receiver down and dialed again. "Let's try Lee Boswell."

Of all the men on the National Union board, Paul knew Boswell best. Maybe he hadn't left home yet.

"Hello, Lee? It's Paul."

"Hey, Paul. How are you?"

"I've got a problem. I'm at the home office with Bill and the rest of the staff. Someone's cleared the place out. I mean *cleared* it. Files, furniture, everything."

A silence fell.

"Lee?"

"I'm — you're certain of that?"

"Lee, you think I'm calling you for a joke? You could play baseball in here. It's wall-to-wall air."

"You got in touch with Basil?"

"Can't raise him."

"Wow." Another silence. "Okay. You stay there. I'll call

around the board and see what I can find out."

"What's happening, Paul?"

This was Bertha Maine, a stout high-heeled lady in formidable blue, with almost the whole staff behind her. Paul held up his hand for quiet and gave a short briefing. He could do little else but to send the staff home — they had nowhere even to sit, let alone any place to work. He arranged to keep in touch with Bill Armor. Paul moved to the door where he stood to watch seventy-five people return to their cars and drive away. The intersection was busier now and they had to line up to leave. After the last car disappeared, Paul lingered by the phone and tried to figure things out.

Autrey's Baptist pastor had introduced Autrey to Paul. It could hardly have been a sounder reference. Autrey, energetic and unflaggingly friendly, had just founded National Union in Alabama. He was looking for what he called "the right person" to handle sales for the company. Paul so impressed him that he immediately offered Paul the exclusive marketing rights on National Union's insurance, plus an option to purchase ten percent of the business. In effect, National Union would supply the product while Paul created an agency to sell it. Both wings of the company's operation would fit in one building. It wasn't the kind of offer you turn down.

Within a year, Paul had recruited eight hundred and thirty-two people. Sales mounted and the cash flowed in. As owner of the agency, 85 percent of the agency's profit came directly under his control. The only others he'd given a cut to — 7.5 percent each — were his immediate deputies Bill Armor and Harold Lanigan. On average, he grossed $20,000 a month in personal earnings — a fortune in the 1950s.

He used the money adventurously. When the agency needed a loan from the Pan American Bank of Miami to advance its agents, Paul immediately signed the note. Autrey suggested they copurchase a fleet of cars, then an airplane, a Cessna 310, the 16th off the production line. Again, Paul signed. He trusted Autrey. They had plenty of money coming in. To seek legal advice over contracts seemed pointless.

Yet intuition told him that something in the business was wrong. He knew a sales boom of the size he'd created could, in theory, result in National Union outselling its surplus — and having insufficient assets to cover claims. But nobody told him to rein in, and he continued to generate new business on the assumption that Autrey had secured adequate funding. In retrospect, such an assumption seemed, at best, ill-founded. Paul, the self-taught businessman, had developed meticulous skills in personal organization. He didn't need formal training to discern the absurdity of Autrey making up the accounts personally and by hand. But so highly did he esteem Autrey that he made no comment. It disturbed Paul that Autrey seemed always late in meeting commitments. Thirty and sixty days late. Paul remembered thinking to himself, *I can't believe anything this sloppy.* Also — why hadn't he seen this at the time? — Autrey never had any money. Autrey's income, also $20,000 a month, slipped through his fingers.

The phone rang.

"Lee?"

"I'm afraid it's bad news, Paul. I've been talking to Stuart Peoples, the CPA."

"And?"

"Apparently Ed Larsen from the Florida Insurance Commission. has been asking Autrey to put up additional assets to cover a surplus shortage."

"How long's that been going on?"

"Months."

"You didn't know?"

"No. Basil and his friends on the board have been playing this pretty close to their vests. But here's the bombshell. Last week Larsen told Autrey that if he didn't comply, the Insurance Commission would close us down."

"*What?*"

"So Autrey decided he'd just move the company back to where it's domiciled in Alabama. The Florida Insurance Commission can't stop him operating up there. Apparently, over the weekend, eight vans came to the office and moved about a million dollars' worth of assets clean out of the state. They even took the stuff in the bank vault. You've been left holding the empty bag."

Paul turned around and kicked the wall, hard. "And Peoples knew about this?"

"I'm afraid so."

"Why didn't anyone tell me?"

"I'm sorry, Paul. I was as much in the dark as you."

"So what am I supposed to do?"

"If I were you, I'd call your lawyer."

From that point on, the agency came apart like a three-dollar suitcase. It had nothing to sell. The bank called in the loans Paul had signed for. He discovered that the down payments for the cars and the Cessna 310 he'd "co-bought" had in fact been made exclusively by him. Autrey had devised a double set of books. The books Autrey showed Paul credited him with the $20,000 for the down payment on the Cessna. In reality, it had been only $10,000. So Paul had been double-charged.

Next day he went to see Claude Pepper, a lawyer who was later to become a U.S. Senator for Florida, and Pepper introduced him to a bright young attorney named Allen Clements. Paul asked what his options were.

After Allen heard the whole story, he told Paul, "You're not a director. You had no involvement in company policy. You can simply give up the agency and go to work for another company whose license is O.K. in Florida. You may get stuck for the loans you signed, but that's about it."

"What happens to the sales people I recruited?"

"They can do the same as you — join another company. Of course, unless somebody picks up National Union the policyholders will lose their investments. But that's not your problem. You didn't run National Union. Autrey did."

"I was the one who recruited the agency staff, and my agency sold the policies."

At that point Clements leaned forward on his elbows and clasped his hands. "Well, your other option is to stay where you are and help straighten out the mess. But I warn you. Nobody will thank you for it. Stick around, Paul, and you'll be the only one who takes the blows."

Paul calculated his assets. First mortgages, property, AT&T bonds, all of them highly liquid. His net worth handily surpassed the million-dollar level. A million dollars he could legally and in all good conscience hold on to.

"Allen, how long do you think it would take to straighten things out, to find somebody willing to put up sufficient capital with the State of Florida?

"You mean pay off the company's creditors and have enough

surplus to be able to continue to write new business?"

"Plus cover the policyholders and find my staff new positions."

"Maybe six months to one year. I don't know. Paul, are you serious? You do this and you could end up broke. Worse than broke."

Paul Meyer thought for a moment, then he said, "So be it."

He walked out of Allen Clements' office, and he and Bill Armor started to work. Somehow they found alternative employment for each of the agents they'd recruited. Somehow they managed to collect $280,000 in premiums which the president of a reinsurance company, Theo Beasley, had written off as uncollectible. With Beasley's cooperation, Paul persuaded one of the shareholders of the Minnesota Mining and Manufacturing Company to put up $600,000 worth of his 3M stock as collateral, guaranteeing National Union's surplus shortage and giving him control of the company.

Several of National Union's directors came under indictment for fraud. Within a year, three of the directors had died from stress-related illnesses, including Stuart Peoples and Basil Autrey. When the legal loose ends were finally tied up, Paul J. Meyer, now 29, emerged from the Miami Courthouse with debts approaching $100,000 and a home he could no longer afford.

He had vindicated himself; his character was unsullied. But would you, like Paul, have chosen this harder road? After all, Paul Meyer had an unassailable right to walk away from National Union. No legal responsibility bound him to his employees or his clients. It is doubtful whether jumping ship would have caused any damage to his reputation. He could have left with his money and a good conscience.

But he didn't. He carried the burdens Autrey and company had loaded on innocent people, and he continued to carry them, voluntarily and with no complaint, for several months — at enormous personal expense. He's never looked back. He's maintained a course of relentless and determined giving, come good or ill, ever since. So much so that he now gives away an average of $342,000 *per month*. For Paul Meyer, giving isn't an occasional spree or an ego-boosting luxury. It's a vocation.

But here's the kicker. Just six months before the fiasco with National Insurance — and influenced by the preaching of his pastor, Bill Hinson — Paul Meyer had significantly increased his regular giving. Why didn't he respond to his loss with an angry expression of betrayal? Why didn't this ordeal sour him permanently on the idea of giving? In the following chapters you'll learn, through Paul's odyssey, the "enlightened self-interest" principles of stewardship. You will understand the faith and commitment and philosophy which inspires his enormous generosity. For Paul Meyer knows that the more he gives, the more God entrusts to him.

2

WHY PAUL J. MEYER IS A SUCCESS

Dear Mr. Meyer,

For the past 18 years Lake Bridge Manor has been my home, and now that I am leaving I would like to take a moment to express to you the appreciation I feel for all the good things you have done for me and for all residents at Lake Bridge Manor. During my tenure here I have seen several owners and numerous managers. Things took a definite up-swing when you became the owner and hired the Carters as managers.

I appreciate you providing the many improvements over the years, a very important one being the additional outdoor lighting you let the Carters install shortly after you hired them. It is so important that single ladies living alone feel safe and secure, and it speaks highly of you knowing you own a property where so many are single ladies.

Most of all, I want you to know how much I appreciated the Carters asking for a reduction in my rent at a time when others were being increased. It was a tremendous help to me when you approved that reduction. Every dollar is vital when you must live on a limited Social Security income. My "Thank You" is heartfelt and sincere. May God bless you.

Yours truly,

Mrs. Sue Matthews.

This letter of thanks — one of a countless number in Paul Meyer's files — witnesses to the simple everyday generosity thatmarks his lifestyle. He gives a young woman a job to keep her from going to jail; he pays for a bereaved mother to visit

Paul preaching the gospel in Japan, November 1989. He is an ambassador for Christ at the global scale.

the Vietnam memorial in Washington, D.C.; he donates $5,000 to a church in Grand Cayman to spend in any way they see fit. He gives substantially to his major philanthropies, and he selects them carefully. Prolific giving so pervades his lifestyle he often has difficulty in remembering having met a person who writes, as Sue Matthews did, a heartfelt letter of thanks.

All this might suggest that Paul has retired from business life to dispense, like Andrew Carnegie, an enormous personal fortune. But that is far from the truth. Paul's businesses span the globe, but he does not aspire to join America's superrich. Nor is he sitting on a pile of capital. He works incredibly hard to generate cash so that he can keep on giving. And he strives to give the money away as fast as he makes it.

Paul has internalized the golden secrets of giving: that it's safe; that it's essential for a full life; that it's fun. His mind-set and experience confute the attitude of those who look upon giving as so much money and time and energy poured down the drain. On the contrary, giving forms the taproot of success. So much so, that Paul Meyer admits to feeling "selfish" giving away so much. To him, philanthropy creates ineffable and sustained pleasure. It produces unspeakable joy.   The desire to give dominates his values, his philosophy of life, his relationship with his family, even his business style.

But particularly when it comes to giving cash, most people seem to see things differently. "I could have used the money for myself," they often say. "But I didn't. I gave it away." They associate giving with self-denial. They describe giving as altruistic, costly, painful. Basically, they have convinced themselves *if it doesn't hurt, it isn't giving.*

Have you never felt that way? If you don't believe me, just go to church and note your feelings as the collection plate comes around.   The writer Earl V. Pierce notes that "The majority of organists play as an offertory something in a minor key, often a veritable dirge, as if to say, 'I sympathize with you. I know how hard this is!'" He recalls once hearing an organist accompany the offering with Chopin's "Funeral March." Pierce concludes that, even among Christians, "giving is looked upon, in the main, as a necessary nuisance from which one is fortunate indeed to escape."[1]

It follows that anyone who gives freely earns lavish applause. Self-sacrifice is accounted noble. "Shall I give to the Lord that which cost me nothing?" asked David in the Old Testament. David, "the man after God's own heart," gave unstintingly. But while we admire him, we also see ourselves as incapable of emulating him.   At first blush, we honestly consider serious giving to lie beyond our reach. How, for instance, do you react to the story of the Good Samaritan?

> *Then Jesus answered and said, "A certain man went down from Jerusalem to Jericho, and fell among thieves, who stripped him of his clothing, wounded him, and departed, leaving him half dead.*
>
> *"Now by chance a certain priest came down that road. And when he saw him, he passed by on the other side. Likewise a certain Levite, when he arrived at the place, came and looked, and passed by on the other side.*
>
> *"But a certain Samaritan, as he journeyed, came where he was. And when he saw him, he had compassion on him, and went to him and bandaged his wounds, pouring on oil and wine; and he set him on his own animal, brought him to an inn, and took care of him"* (Luke 10:30-34).

Nobody forced the Samaritan to stop and help the injured man. His compassion shocks us because the injured man was a Jew, and a Jew would have been the Samaritan's natural enemy. What could the Samaritan hope to gain by "doing the honorable thing"? Nothing obvious. So we call him a "good man," by which we mean "not like us."

But is serious giving really beyond us?

Paul Meyer, whose giving is enormous relative to his income, disavows the suggestion that he is extraordinary — that nobody else, with a little thought and application, could do what he has done. His life and example challenge us to go back and see more clearly what giving is all about. Here are the lessons.

1. Understand the paradox of giving

There is a paradox at the heart of giving.

Start with the Biblical view of human nature. Take an average person and perform a kind of psychological biopsy. You will discover that he, or she, is basically, consistently, and irretrievably self-centered.

Why, then, does anybody give? After all, life is about competition, conflict, self-preservation, survival. "Two companies and one contract," "two suitors and one girl," and "two applicants and one job": life abounds with occasions where demand outstrips supply. Competition emerges because each player looks after his own interests first. And everybody wants to win.

I ask again: why does anybody give? Here's the point. Any rational person will give willingly provided he can be convinced of resulting and larger benefits. In fact all of us give every day, spontaneously, unconsciously, because through giving we expect to gain. We give in order to *receive* from giving.

Cooperative behavior, then, doesn't run on altruism any more than competition does. I give to receive. I pay taxes because taxation finances the police, and the police protect my property. I sacrifice my time for an employer because I want money for food. In other words, my motive for cooperating remains anchored in concern for my own welfare. There's a name for this: *enlightened self-interest.*

Naturally you can find people who derive little obvious benefit from federal taxation, and others who work voluntarily. But in the last analysis, they still act out of enlightened self-interest — to gain an advantage or avoid a loss. Every taxpayer knows the IRS will penalize him if he doesn't pay up; the voluntary worker, while not receiving a paycheck, nevertheless gains self-esteem, reputation, experience, satisfaction.

This truth applies universally. Scripture assumes that people act from self-interest (why else does the Law of the Old Testament link obedience to blessing, and the Gospel of the New Testament link repentance to salvation?). Observation of human behavior confirms our willingness to make even big personal sacrifices after a quick cost-benefit calculation has shown us it's advantageous. In the hard-bitten realms of business and politics, enlightened self-interest is taken for granted. It may be, as Andrew Carnegie suggested, "a nobler ideal that man should labor, not for himself alone, but in and for a brotherhood of his fellows." But the ideal does not build railroads. To expect men to give their time and energy without a perceived benefit to themselves, "necessitates the changing of human nature. . . . It is not practicable in our day or in our age."[2]

Even a mother's love for her children involves enlightened self-interest. The children give her a role, status, stimulation, happiness, future security. It is this meeting of her own needs, as much as parent-child bonding, that explains her unwillingness to relinquish the child, though the child sustains a disfiguring injury or turns out to be a thoughtless brute. Parenthood is not an act of unstinting self-sacrifice. It may not turn out, as one person has said, quite the way it looks in the brochure; but it brings special rewards, and a thousand years from now the dreams of the average couple exchanging vows at the altar will still feature a beaming, drooling infant.

Let me press the argument to its conclusion: not even a willingness to lay down one's life for others can be separated from enlightened self-interest. "If I should die," asks Rupert Brook's soldier-poet, "think only this of me, that there is some corner of a foreign field that is forever England. . . ." Clearly he views the life laid down in battle as an accomplishment; the G.I. killed in action receives his nation's highest esteem and gratitude — hence the worth attached to heroic last stands. Were those at the Alamo or Little Big Horn mindful *only* of their patriotic duty? I find that hard to believe. To die purposefully and willingly may be the ultimate self-sacrifice; but it guarantees you a place in history.

This is taking things to extremes, to be sure, and no doubt most of us can think of at least one action in which a person has shown himself completely and inexplicably selfless.   But even assuming these cases stand up under closer scrutiny, they remain exceptional. In general, people check out the consequences of a decision to ensure some prospect of advantage. You may heartily dislike walking the dog, but you console yourself with the thought that walking at least gives you exercise, and that you can pick up the morning paper while you're out.

This being the case, it's hardly surprising that someone asking you for money will try to persuade you first of all that giving is to your advantage. A prosperity preacher will claim (without blinking) that God repays you double, triple, or quadruple, for every donation you send in. It's a sure-fire heavenly speculation with the dividends paid in hard cash (none of this vague "spiritual blessing" nonsense), though guaranteed, of course, only on condition that you open an account with that particular preacher.   Pay up, and claim your reward.

You find that distasteful? I do. Yet prosperity preachers survive and occasionally get rich because their message contains a grain of truth.   Something in the organization of God's universe tends to reward giving, to make it worthwhile even in blunt cost-benefit terms. Not that the desire for worldly gain is the worthiest motive for philanthropy. In that sense, Paul Meyer remains exceptional in both the degree and the freedom of his generosity. He gives without thought of his own well-being and is therefore about as close to genuine altruism as a human being is likely to get. Yet Paul will be the first to admit that generosity brings certain personal benefits. He believes strongly that God repays and rewards a giver. And he finds the experience of giving hugely pleasurable. For Paul, as for anybody else, the paradox of giving holds true: giving *pays.*

But why?

2. Understand investment and return

The writer and philosopher Ralph Waldo Emerson once heard a sermon on the Last Judgment.

The argument ran like this. At the moment, bad people have a great time, while good people are miserable. But good people shouldn't despair. When the last trump sounds and the wheat and tares are gathered in, the situation will be reversed. From then on into the deepest reaches of Eternity, good people will have a great time, and bad people will be miserable. Therefore, since Eternity will last a lot longer than the present dispensation, one is, on balance, better off being good than bad.

The congregation noted this soberly. Emerson, though, nearly suffered an apoplectic fit. The preacher seemed to imply that God repaid the good with the same kinds of luxury — "bank-stock and doubloons, venison and champagne" — that foreshadowed the bad's damnation. "The legitimate inference the disciple would draw was . . .'You sin now, we shall sin by and by; we would sin now, if we could; not being successful we expect our revenge tomorrow.'"[3]

"The fallacy," concludes Emerson — and one can imagine him shaking his head as he left the church — "lay in the immense concession that the bad are successful: that justice is not done now."

In reply, he sat down and penned the essay titled "Compensation." It's a stiff read. But Emerson's point is this: the world is so constructed that every action you perform bounces back at you like a ball. Borrow money, and you incur a debt. Venture nothing, gain nothing. Live honorably, and you will be honored. Love, and others will love you. "Commit a crime, and the earth is made of glass."

He ties up the loose ends rather too neatly. Still, we can see what he's driving at. Give and it will be given back to you; take, and what you have taken will be taken away. Whether you give or take, you are paid back in kind. The law isn't immutable, nor is it exact, but it seems roughly to hold.

We could express Emerson's idea of compensation in simpler terms by saying that:

INVESTMENT   ⇨   RETURN

So, for instance:

Give money	⇨	Receive goods
Invest money	⇨	Build savings
Plan route	⇨	Reach destination
Study drawing	⇨	Improve drawing skills
Follow recipe	⇨	Produce meal

*Paul as a body-builder at age 18. Physical fitness was
one of his earliest goals.*

The logic is self-evident: we expend our resources of money, energy, and time to achieve a given result. We do it consciously. We do it constantly. And we know the value of sound investments and sound procedures. Go to the store without your wallet, and you won't be able to buy anything. Leave the dinner in the oven too long, and it will burn. Fail to consult the map, and you will get lost. Neglect to save, and you will limit your financial options later in life.

The same investment-return effect works over far longer periods of time. For instance, do you think of Mozart as a musical genius? Yet according to the British Professor of Psychology John Sloboda, "It is a myth that some people can sit down at the age of five and play beautifully . . . musicians are made not born. Even Mozart had to put in the hours."[4] Recent studies show that if children accumulate about 5,000 hours of practice before the age of 18 — that's just over an hour a day—they should be good enough to get into music college. A competent amateur would need between 1,000 and 2,000 hours. Reaching world-class standard takes a gruelling 10,000 hours. The message? "You don't have to be good early on to achieve a reasonable standard later in life. You don't have to be anything special to be a musician." What you *do* need is investment.

At this level, investment thinking means goal-directed behavior. The entrepreneur deliberately practices self-denial (postponing gratification) in order to accumulate capital. The speculator deliberately risks funds in order to attract a high return. An athlete trains daily to win the hundred meters, a mountaineer to conquer Everest. Students invest years of study to receive a degree or a diploma.

This is thoroughly Biblical. The Bible tells us: "He who sows sparingly will also reap sparingly, and he who sows bountifully will also reap bountifully." Plant barley, you get barley. Plant grass, you get grass. "Whatever a man sows, that he will also reap" (Galatians 6:7; I Corinthians 6:9).

And, of course, the principle of investment and return underlies everything we do. That's why we need to understand it. Even the most complex procedures can be broken down into sequences of investments and returns — building a house, gaining a promotion, landing a manned space vehicle on Mars. It's by breaking big tasks down into collections of small tasks that we get them done.

Say you want to move. You're required to make two major investments to accomplish the move: (1) you need to select the

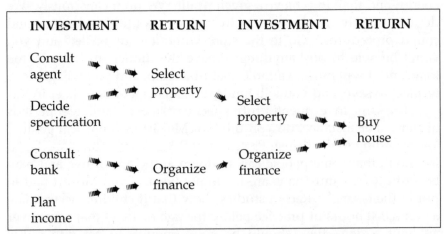

Figure 2.1: Housebuying in terms of investment and return

property, and (2) you need to arrange the financing to purchase it. These investments, however, are themselves returns resulting from other, earlier investments. To select a property, you need not only to find houses for sale, but to decide what kind of house you want. To put together finance you need both to plan and to borrow. Expressed in terms of investment and return, house-buying begins to look something like *Figure 2.1*.

Does the investment-return principle always work? The answer is no. It's a fact of life that every kind of investment carries risks. A back injury may prevent me from becoming a professional football star; the promotion I have labored to win may be handed to the boss's nephew; my stocks may plunge. That means you have to plan and choose your investments carefully. Paul J. Meyer studies all the available data before investing; and if that data isn't available, he falls back on his informed intuition or the spiritual conviction that a certain course is God's will. He also practices the patience of Job. For that is the other danger with investment — that we lose heart through impatience. Paul Meyer knows that any one crop may suffer a flood, a drought, a pestilence; but he also knows that a farmer will see many seasons, and that in the long run a farmer who sows consistently will reap plentifully. He takes the long view. So have patience. Given time, the law of reciprocity will not be denied.

3. Understand the boomerang effect

A real estate agent by the name of Abner Bartlett once arrived in Philadelphia for a few days rest with his wife. Every major hotel except one turned him away: no rooms. The Bellevue gave him a room. The Bellevue had only twenty-four rooms. It was a neat, compact, red-brick building on the northeast corner of Broad and Walnut, only recently furnished with an elevator. Like all the other hotels in town it was full. Bartlett was ready to step out into the street again, when the manager added, "But we can accommodate you."

"I thought you were fully booked," replied Bartlett.

"We are. However you and Mrs. Bartlett may have the use of my private suite."

This made such an impression on Bartlett that he called the incident to mind a few years later when his friend and client William

Waldorf Astor consulted him about the use of a property on New York's Thirty-third Street.

"I think that we will build that hotel," Bartlett said slowly. He and Astor had discussed the idea of a five-star hotel in New York several times before.

Astor seemed dubious. "It will never pay in a location like that."

"Oh yes," said Bartlett. "It will pay. I have thought the thing all out, and I am now positive that it will pay."

Astor considered this for a few moments, then turned to the real estate agent and asked, "Have you got a man to look after a hotel like that, if we should decide to build it?"

Bartlett replied firmly: "I have the man."

So it was that George Boldt of the Bellevue became general manager of the Waldorf Astoria.[5]

I have had similar experiences. I checked in with a business party at the Bali Hyatt on the island of Bali in Indonesia a few years ago. A handsome man, about 35, whose face caught my attention, said, "Dr. Haggai, welcome." Then I remembered who he was. I had known him when he was a teenager hustling bags at the old Intercontinental Hotel in Singapore.

He said, "I told my staff that you are our guest. We have assigned you a complimentary suite, the finest in the hotel." Then he turned to all the people with me and said, "This man treated me as well as he treated the head of the corporation when he used to come to Singapore. I could never do enough for him."

On another occasion, in 1981, I was at the airport in Brisbane, Australia, to catch a flight to Sydney. A vicious storm created havoc at the airport. There were delays. One Ansett Airline flight had already been canceled, and people were angry. They were rubbishing the manager at the Ansett counter, being inexcusably rude.

I walked up quietly and said, "I'm so sorry that these people are rubbishing you. I'm sure they don't mean what they are saying. They're frustrated. Is there anything I can do to help?"

The clerk said, "I'm just sorry you are not going to get into Sydney tonight."

I said, "No matter. I understand perfectly. These things happen."

Less than a year later, I was at the same airport about to board a plane when the attendant said, "You have been upgraded to first class." I was surprised. Then, with a grin, the attendant said, "Mr. Higgins, the manager, said you had been such a gentleman to him last year when he thought people were going to do him physical harm, he wanted to express his appreciation."

We are dealing here with a different kind of investment-return mechanism; the ball still bounces back, but from a different wall. We are looking not at the translation of effort into the accomplishing of goals, but at the boomerang effect of *reciprocity*:

INVESTMENT   ⇨   RETURN

Doing a favor   ⇨   Receiving a favor

We talk about "one good turn deserving another," and about "owing a favor," implying that in our relations with others we keep mental balance sheets. If I lend you $100 today, I will confidently expect you to lend me $100 tomorrow. If you *don't*, I will think you insensitive and ungrateful. In fact your awareness of this expectation — of the deficit on your balance sheet — will be one of the main pressures on you to grant my request. Generosity comes back like a boomerang. Of course, it may not be that the next customer you serve a hamburger will return at closing time in a gold-plated limo to install you as CEO of McDonald's. Nevertheless the principle is true. Practice decent behavior — invest kindness — and you'll tend to invite decent behavior in the other person. You want me to buy you lunch tomorrow? Buy me lunch today.

A few years ago, Shades Mountain Baptist Church in Birmingham, Alabama, elected to build a new sanctuary. The pastor, Dr. Charles T. Carter, started a campaign to raise the money. At a service soon after, a young church member and singer named Becky Seay made an announcement. She and her husband, she said, did not have any money for the building — they gave regularly to the church, and couldn't increase their contribution. "But I do have," she added, holding up a string of jewelry, "this diamond necklace. I'm asking the church to sell it, and to put the money from the sale into the church building fund."

A friend of Paul Meyer, J. I. "Mac" McCormick, belonged to the same congregation. Immediately after the service, Mac took Charles Carter aside and told him not to sell the necklace. "Get it appraised," he said, "then let me know and I'll write you a check for that amount. Afterwards, put the necklace back in the safe until I tell you what to do with it."

Carter did this. Several months later, at Christmas, Mac called him and asked him to wrap the necklace up as a gift and return it to Becky Seay. "Don't tell her who made the payment. Just say an interested donor was happy to put the amount in the fund, and equally happy to return her gift."

I could quote other stories about McCormick. This particular one, of course, illustrates the truth that "one good turn deserves another." Becky Seay had not expected to see her necklace again; and Mac certainly hadn't returned it with the expectation of being rewarded. Yet, many years later, it was Becky Seay who accepted a request to sing at his memorial service. Giving stimulates giving.

Sometimes, of course, people invest deliberately, even manipulatively. The writer of Proverbs attests the effectiveness of this when he tells us "a soft answer turns away wrath" (Proverbs 15:1). So, too, does the character known as the "unjust steward" in Christ's parable (Luke 16:1-8):

> And He also said to His disciples: "There was a certain rich man who had a steward, and an accusation was brought to him that this man was wasting his goods. So he called him and said to him, 'What is this I hear about you? Give an account of your stewardship, for you can no longer be steward.'
>
> "Then the steward said within himself, 'What shall I do? For my master is taking the stewardship away from me. I cannot dig; I am ashamed to beg. I have resolved what to do, that when I am put out of the stewardship, they may receive me into their houses.' So he called every one of his master's debtors to him, and said to the first, 'How much do you owe my master? And he said, 'A hundred measures of oil.' So he said to him, 'Take your bill, and sit down quickly and write fifty.' Then he said to another, 'And how much do you owe?' So he said, 'A hundred measures of wheat.' And he said to him, 'Take your bill, and write eighty.'
>
> "So the master commended the unjust steward because he had dealt shrewdly. For the sons of this world are more shrewd in their generation than the sons of light."

The parable often baffles interpreters, because in commending the unjust steward, Christ seems to applaud dishonesty. In fact, the parable focuses on the principle of reciprocity. Knowing he's about to be terminated, the unjust steward slashes the creditors' debts. He does the creditors a favor. In so doing, he transforms a portion of the financial debt into a moral debt to himself. From now on they will "owe him one."

People in employment do exactly this when they try to "keep on the right side of the boss." They calculate that being nice to the boss will encourage the boss to be nice to them. With good reason, apparently. A recent survey of 108 bank employees (using MIBOS, the Measure of Ingratiatory Behaviors in Organizational Settings) showed that "yes-men" were approved of by their superiors, obtain positive assessment reports, and are more likely to be promoted.[6]

But the same effect will occur without conscious guidance. For example, Paul Meyer's son Larry called him one day and said, "I just had dinner in Dallas with a man by the name of Gary Richardson — a friend of one of my employees."

Richardson had asked Larry, "Hey, you wouldn't by chance be Paul Meyer's son, would you?"

Larry replied, "Yes, how did you know him?"

"I worked for him 30 years ago," said Richardson. "I sure would like to see him again. I've been wanting to do it for a long time, and I've just been putting it off. Could you mention to him that I'd like to give him a call, and go down to Waco and tell him thank you?"

When Richardson finally came to Waco he said to Paul, "You don't remember me, do you?"

"No," said Paul.

"I used to work for you. I heard you speak, and one of your other people recruited me. But when I got your plan of action and filled it out, I realized SMI wasn't my calling. So I quit working for you and went back to school and got a law degree. I made twenty million dollars last year. I'm one of the top-paid lawyers in the U.S. And I've set nine United States records in the courthouse."

The amazing twist to the story is that Gary Richardson turned up just when Paul was looking for a lawyer with his legal expertise to represent him in a case. So he said, "Would you like to do some work for me?"

"Sure," said Richardson.

"I'm afraid I can't pay the kind of fees you're used to."

But Richardson waved his hand. "Don't worry about it," he said. "It would be a pleasure to help you after all you've done to influence my life."

The boomerang effect, however, doesn't end with tit-for-tat transactions, bouncing back and forth like a tennis ball between the same two individuals. Sometimes it operates indirectly:

INVESTMENT   ⇨ RETURN
Giving directions ⇨ Being given directions

It's ridiculous to believe that the Scot who asks you for directions in Chicago will happen to be there five years later when you need directions in Edinburgh. Nevertheless, we help others, partly at least, because we wish others to help us. We constantly chip in our quota of generosity and decency, expecting to receive the same in kind even from people we've never met before. We observe certain common courtesies — saying "thank you" and "please," for example — and if the new girl at the checkout gives us a scowl instead of wishing us a nice day we feel she's not paying her dues.

Reciprocity, in fact, is like a kind of credit system. We all make sure our giving and receiving falls roughly into balance, though we may give and receive from scores of different people. When your parents taught you to say "How do you do?" and to keep your mouth closed when you eat, they were raising you to give to others. The expectation being that, on balance, others would give to you in return.

The psychologists call this "prosocial behavior." We call a person back in a restaurant if he's left his gloves on the seat. We drive on the correct side of the road. We stop to help an elderly person who has fallen on the sidewalk. And because we all agree that giving is good, we keep one another in line. We notice and disapprove when somebody else breaks the rules — the dangerous driver, the bad-mannered child, the freeloader, the boor, the faultfinder. So much so that if we visit a country with different customs — where, for instance, it is thought appropriate to barge in instead of standing in line — our first reaction is to say the locals are inconsiderate and rude.

Then, note this: investment lasts, and benefits people you will never see. On a visit to the People's Republic of China in 1984, my wife and I joined a luncheon party in the Shanghai Hotel. As we stepped into the top-floor restaurant my wife fell and injured her wrist. It hurt so much we thought she'd broken it. Fortunately, the party included a doctor, and after making a quick examination he said, "Let's get her downstairs. My hospital is just across the road."

I remember crossing the busy Shanghai street and entering the hospital compound, thankful that advanced medical facilities were located so close by. Only on the way out of the medical compound did I notice a plaque outside the hospital's largest building. It read: BUILT BY JOHN D. ROCKEFELLER.

4. Understand God's challenge to the giver

On their own, however, investment and return and the boomerang effect of reciprocity do not fully explain the degree of Paul Meyer's success in giving. Why not?

Ask Paul Meyer why he gives and he will give you a simple answer: stewardship. "God is the owner of this business," he says, "I simply work for Him." Stewardship is the explicit acknowledgement that your financial resources belong to God, and that you only manage them on God's behalf. Paul points out that giving is the only issue in the Bible on which God challenges the believer to put Him to the test. He *dares* a Christian to give. Two of Paul's favorite Scriptures on money and stewardship are:

> Bring all the tithes into the storehouse, that there may be food in my house, and prove me now in this . . . if I will not open for you the windows of heaven and pour out for you such blessing that there will not be room enough to receive it (Malachi 3:10).

> Give, and it will be given to you; good measure, pressed down, shaken together, and running over will be put into your bosom. For with the same measure that you use, it will be measured back to you (Luke 6:38).

God throws down the gauntlet. He instructs us to try out stewardship. He asks us to put ourselves and everything we have directly into His hands. Paul Meyer tests this promise daily, and he wants to make this demonstration of faith a testimony to others. Ask him how he would like to be remembered in his hometown and he replies, "As a Christlike person — a Christian who did not just think like a Christian and believe like a Christian, but acted like one toward those less fortunate — who cared not only in thought but in action. I would like to be a role model to my family and others as far as stewardship of time, talent, and money is concerned."

Paul Meyer's firm grasp of stewardship underlies his entire business style. He fiercely maintains the priority of giving against periodic business failure and often heavy debt repayments. Faith drives him on when reasonable caution might hold another man back. He recalls a conversation with his wife, Jane, in the shadow of a crisis:

"The tax law changed, and the real estate was overbuilt. We talked about what was going to happen, and I said, 'Look, we took a chance; we are entrepreneurs; so we made our bed. We sleep in it. We have to accept personal responsibility for what happened.'

"But here's what is significant. During that whole time, my giving went like this. . . .'" He traces a steadily rising line in the air. "And some of the creditors were not happy with me. They said, 'I understand you give a lot to charity; you'd do better if you paid off these notes.' I said, 'Wrong. I pay the Lord first and pay you second. How do you like that?' They just did not understand." (Still less did they understand how he could live by a rule like that and *never once be late on a payment*.)

Becoming a giver, then, demands the cultivation of your spiritual resources. Your trust in God. Your inner strength. Your ability to maintain a course that others have forsaken. Your moral fiber. Your commitment — stunningly illustrated in Paul Meyer — to honor pledges in faith that God will supply the means to pay them. Ultimately, your ability to internalize the truth that God will supply:

> *Be anxious for nothing, but in everything in prayer and supplication with thanksgiving, let your requests be made known to God; and the peace of God, which surpasses all understanding, will guard your hearts and minds through Christ Jesus (Philippians 4:6-7).*

3

GET READY TO GIVE

Paul J. Meyer shuns displays of flamboyant generosity. I've known him nearly a quarter of a century. Dr. William M. (Bill) Hinson has known him for 38 years. We both agree that Paul finds exposure of his giving somewhat distasteful. He agrees to it — in this book, for example — only because he's finally been convinced his experience may challenge others. They will, in turn, bless others and thus be blessed.

Eleven years ago I wrote a book about Guy W. Rutland's giving. It took me nine years to get his permission. He reluctantly agreed when I convinced him (1) that giving in the Bible was always done publicly, and (2) that his story could encourage others to follow suit. Within a year of publication, a Cincinnati businessman and his wife read the Rutland story and decided to give more than $2 million of their $8-million estate to Christian causes.

1. Understand why most people don't give

So why do we need encouragement to give, when the rewards of giving are plain to see?

I think there are two reasons.

First, we mismanage our resources by failing to think out clearly what investments are necessary to achieve a given return.

There's a parable Jesus told about five wise and five foolish virgins. They were waiting to accompany the bridegroom into the wedding feast. He was late, and by the time he finally turned up at midnight the virgins' lamps were almost burned out. The wise virgins had anticipated the delay and brought along extra supplies of oil to keep their lamps burning; the foolish ones had not. Consequently, while the wise virgins were joining the party, the foolish virgins were walking up and down trying to find a shop to buy more oil.

Proverbial wisdom? Yet it's amazing how sparingly we apply it. In general we think far more about returns than investments, far more about what we want to get *out* of an opportunity than what we will have to put *in*. We dream about getting a high-paying position. We bask in the anticipated delight of a big income and increased social status. We are far less inclined to invest essential time in researching the company and preparing ourselves for evaluation.

It's mismanagement. Our failure in strategic planning does us in. We resemble the famous professor of history at Oxford who once turned up on his neighbor's doorstep asking how to boil an egg. He knew what he wanted for breakfast, but he hadn't a clue how to cook it.

Strangely, sloppiness over investment can hit us hardest in our finances. Unquestionably, long-term financial security should take priority over planning next year's vacation. Yet, according to Paul Meyer who has been in the behavioral modification business for 35 years, most people spend more time planning their vacation than they do their finances. They devote hours to reading travel brochures and minutes to planning their savings. It's not that they don't want to be well-off. It's not even that the movements of the financial markets defy understanding. They simply lack the will or confidence to master the "investment" side of a big issue: what they must give in order to receive. Consequently they drift along, carried along by financial currents they cannot control. They neglect to cultivate the discipline of investment thinking necessary to gain the returns they dream of. They stop with the dreams — houses, cars, clothes, balmy poolsides in Florida. Their wish list remains unfulfilled. They fail to come anywhere near achieving their full potential.

Second, we suffer from myopia by looking only for direct and immediate returns on our investment.

Myopia means shortsightedness: figuratively, lack of foresight or discernment. We can see the value of putting $200 a month into savings; what we stand to gain from giving the same amount to charity, however, is not immediately obvious. We can see no return. Therefore we refuse to invest.

It's not hard to see the result of this. By putting on blinders we limit our choices. We say "It's not worth the effort," or "I'd be wasting my time," or "Nothing will ever come of it." Whole swatches of potentially enriching investment are simply cut away and discarded.

Our social prejudices are notorious in this respect. We starve a particular relationship of our time and energy because we think the other person "isn't our type." Yet what wealth, what support, what enjoyment we miss by this kind of self-imposed limitation. Many young people do the same with their schooling. How often have you heard a teenager say, "What's the point of a college degree?"

That's myopia of the clearest kind. The person refuses to invest because he, or she, can't see what the return is going to be. And as for giving financially, the idea that philanthropy could actually *pay* conflicts so sharply with our culture's received wisdom that we relegate it to the twilight zone of harebrained optimism and prosperity theology. And yet the principle of investment and return operates in the area of giving as it does in every other field.

2. Understand what it means to succeed

In this book I focus particularly on the issue of financial giving, on philanthropy.

I do that because giving money strikes many as crucial; it's a discipline ordinary people seem to find extremely difficult. But I do not wish to give the impression that one should gloss over other kinds of investment and return. It's just that literally thousands of books are written about the investment of time, influence, energy, and abilities. How many books have you read about giving? How many success magazines give even a passing mention to the importance of giving as an essential ingredient of success? Return, for a moment, to the story I began in Chapter One.

After the final settlement of the National Union disaster, Paul Meyer descended the steps of Miami courthouse heavily in debt.

Today he can see the funny side. "You know, I say that life is like baseball. You win some; you lose some; and in some you get rained out. This time I'd lost it all. The ironic thing was, a few months before all this blew up I'd just begun to tithe. So I was thinking, 'This is a blessing from God? This is what I get for starting to tithe? This is the payoff? Boy, He must be trying to tell me something!'"

What happened next, however, brings a broad grin to Paul's face.

"There I was, dumped on my backside.   I'd lost my bank account; I'd lost my stocks and securities; I'd lost my Cadillacs, my airplanes, and my house. I had nothing.   And I'm standing by the courthouse and Claude Pepper comes up — already a famous lawyer, later to become a United States senator. He put his arms around me and says 'You are the richest young man I know.'   I replied, 'Thanks, Sir. Would you mind explaining that to me?'"

Pepper promptly obliged. "Paul," he said, "you could have walked away from this mess and kept your personal fortune intact. You may not have any money left, but you have something of far greater worth. You have integrity."

What do you think? You've probably heard remarks like that before. Is integrity small change from a million dollars — or is it a fair swap?

Conventional wisdom says "small change." It so states not only because it's myopic (seeing only immediate returns) but because in American culture money has exaggerated value.   From such a viewpoint, sacrificing not only your time, but your whole fortune to bail out people who will never pay you back appears foolhardy. You are frittering away your most valuable asset.

Have you ever wondered why the rich can be so stingy? That's the reason. If you study the grandest social season (1882-83) as recorded in the pages of the *New York Tribune,* you will learn that out of 849 social events (excluding weddings) only 30 were organized for the benefit of charity. Three generations of Jacobs and Vanderbilts left less than 2.5 percent of their estates to philanthropic causes. Of five men who acquired fortunes in the range of $21-38 million — Collis P. Huntingdon, the stock speculator John W. ("Bet a Million") Gates, William C. Whitney, and J.P. Morgan — all spent lavishly on townhouses, country estates, yachts, racing, and art.   But only Morgan made sizeable donations while still alive. Significantly, Huntingdon remarked, "I'll never be remembered for the money I've given away." Dead right. He wasn't.

Possibly the strangest tale of stinginess is that of the "witch of Wall Street," Hattie Green. Born into a wealthy household, she became the richest woman of her time, with a fortune approaching $100 million in real estate and railway stock. Yet she gave sparingly to charity both before and after her death. More remarkably, she herself wore old clothes, lived in cheap hotels and, when her son succumbed to an infection, refused to pay for medical assistance with the result that the boy lost a leg.

Don't get me wrong. I'm not condemning wealth. I believe that the well-being of a nation depends on the freedom of its citizens to create wealth and to enjoy the fruit of their labor. I endorse wholeheartedly the words attributed to Abraham Lincoln, "You can't enrich the poor by impoverishing the rich." And although it's among the rich that America's obsession with money and material goods is most glaringly conspicuous, I'm also proud to say that many rich people excel in generosity.

Nor am I claiming that the wealthy fail to observe the principle of investment and return. Successful entrepreneurs grasp the principle firmly as it applies to organization and management. That's what gives them their competitive edge. The ability to invest time and money and relationships productively is what "successful" (here meaning "celebrated") leaders are admired for. It's what the thousand and one personal success books buckling the shelves of the average American bookstore help others to cultivate.

Yet Claude Pepper's assertion continues to challenge us. Rich or poor, a person's life-aims reveal the most important thing about him. It's worth reflecting, therefore, on what your life-aims really are. What do you *mean* when you say you want to be successful? What precise destination are you trying to reach? And am I just copping out if I insist that integrity is as valuable as money?

Legend has it that when Lincoln worked as a young lawyer in Springfield, a farmer came to see him. This farmer was famous for his bragging, and Lincoln decided it was high time somebody put him in his place.

Lincoln remarked that they'd just put up the hay on his farm.

The Farmer cocked an eyebrow. "So, you got a farm, then, Mr. Lincoln."

"Yes, I sure do."

"Was it a big hay crop?"

Clearly the farmer was anxious in case somebody else's crop had exceeded his. Lincoln replied, "Yep, sure was. Real big hay crop this year."

"So exactly how much hay do you have?" pressed the farmer.

"Well. . ." drawled Lincoln, casting a lingering glance out the window. "I don't know just how much we have. They stacked up all they could outdoors, and put the rest in the barn."

For a long time, then, Western society has tended to reduce "success" to money. Of two managers, the one with the higher income will be thought the more successful. Of two drivers, the more successful will be seen as the one driving the Rolls Royce.

Strangely, this distinction of the haves from the have-nots applies at all points on the socioeconomic scale. It not only separates the respectably poor from the destitute, but also establishes degrees of wealth among the rich. When the celebrated banker J.P. Morgan died in 1914, he left an estate of around $80 million — a sizeable cache even by today's standards. "And to think," commented John D. Rockefeller, "he wasn't even a wealthy man."

However you define success, then, you don't have it in society's eyes unless you have a lot of money. But of course the dollars by which our culture measures success actually signify something quite different. Strip success down to its essentials and you'll find, not dollars, but other desires which we expect dollars to fulfill.

The New Testament bulges with wealthy characters — Nicodemus, Zacchaeus, the rich young ruler, and the rich fool of Christ's parable — whose wealth left them unfulfilled. And no doubt Aristotle in his *Nicomachean Ethics* wasn't the first to point out that "The life of money-making is one undertaken under compulsion, and wealth is evidently not the good we are seeking; for it is merely useful and for the sake of something else."[7]

What that "something else" consists of, however, invites debate. We might describe it (though perhaps not very accurately) by using words like *happiness, fulfillment, peace,* or — to borrow from the Hebrew — *shalom.* Earle Pierce uses the term "blessedness":

> Blessedness is something more than happiness. It has to do with the soul. Happiness depends upon the propitious "hap," the comfortable circumstance, the easy environment, the auspicious earthly experience. Blessedness points to well-being within. It is the life of the spirit. It can gladly associate with happiness, but it is not extinguished by pain. Blessedness is perfect poise and peace, a quality and richness of soul that is unaffected by the wind and wave of adverse circumstance.[8]

It's by no means certain — indeed it is frankly unlikely —that money will achieve such things. During the years when immense fortunes were being racked up in America, "most multimillionaires endured damaged egos. Nervous breakdowns, family conflicts, alcoholism, and suicide intruded the renaissance palaces along New York's Upper Fifth Avenue or Chicago's Near North Side."[9]

At the same time, as numerous folk songs will tell you, soul-warming satisfaction can be yours without spending a single cent. Witness the words of one television repairman:

> If I went to a house, to repair their television, and it wasn't working when I went there — especially if there were children there — and after I repaired it and I left, there was a family there happy — happy with the work that I'd done — that made me happy. I can come home at night, knowing that I've made several families happy. Whereas I go to do a day's work in the mill, and what have I achieved? All I've achieved is money.[10]

Modern America makes the error of King Midas. Nothing has real value unless it can be changed into gold, into dollars. Yet as Midas discovered to his cost, money in itself is nothing. You can't talk to it. You can't eat it. And although in large enough amounts it will buy three French chateaux and access to an exclusive social set, it will not secure loyalty or respect or love. In the end, life consists of more than money. Have you ever heard of a dying millionaire asking his accountant, "Bring me my net worth statement and put it under my head to comfort me in my dying hour?"

If we want to talk about success, therefore, I suggest that we will have to talk about it not just in one, but in five categories. I call them the FIRST life-areas:

FINANCE	(Capital, income, credit)
INFORMATION	(Intellect, training, knowledge)
RELATIONSHIPS	(Personal relationships, contacts, faith)
SPIRIT	(Creativity, devotion, inner strength)
TIME/ENERGY	(Available time, stamina, health)

I can succeed financially. But I can also succeed informationally (through learning), in my relationships (through my ability to cultivate family and make friends and exert influence), in my spirit (through my religious devotion, creativity, and inner resources), and in my available time/energy (through good mental and physical health).

Whether I can succeed in all FIRST life-areas at the same time and to the same degree raises a moot point. All too often, home life, health, and creativity are sacrificed to the demands of the job. And not infrequently, spiritual success — the kind a Mother Teresa of Calcutta or a Dr. Han Kyung Chik of Korea reveals — involves a redefinition of financial wealth in terms most of us would find hard to stomach.

Be that as it may, the truly successful person surely succeeds across the board. No matter how great the distinction you achieve in your chosen field, if your home life collapses into sullenness and strife, you *know* you are not succeeding. No matter how great a mother or homemaker you are, if you feel deeply unfulfilled, you *know* you are not succeeding.

The successful person reveals a full-orbed life that you could describe in one word: whole.

3. Understand how to be whole

So how do you achieve such "wholeness"? I assert that nongivers never attain this glorious status, this zest, this comprehensive vitality in living.

You can't buy wholeness. You can neither snatch it, nail it down, nor mark it with your branding iron and pen it in your corral. It has to do with fulfilling potential in *all* areas, becoming more fully alive, more balanced. It has to be a feature of your entire life-management.

But let's play with definitions for a moment.

We might define success as follows: *approaching the outer limits of your potential in every area.*

Notice first the word: "approaching." To succeed isn't only to achieve a given goal, but to be moving toward it in the manner you've planned. "I have succeeded" suggests that a particular return has been attained, and that everything preceding this point falls short of success. The present tense — "I am succeeding" — perhaps gives a more accurate flavor of what success is all about. It goes on. It progresses, builds on itself.

So far so good. But the idea of success in itself does not

distinguish good methods from bad. In fact, in a highly competitive society like ours, many pundits promote the idea that you succeed *against* others, not *with* them.

Of course there's nothing wrong with competition: most of our business and sport is built on it. But competition has a weakness. It tends to foster a spirit of aggressive acquisition. Our culture tells us loud and clear that takers win, not givers. Where "nothing gets handed to you on a plate," the people with full plates are the ones gutsy enough to go out and fill them. Our very language reflects this: you *take* a job, *take* advantage of opportunity, *take* your chances, *take* the prize.

By the same token, most people assume that once they've earned their money, they have the right to dispose of it exactly as they want. Nobody else can tell them how to spend it. According to this philosophy, you might enjoy financial wealth in a society where many suffer disadvantage, chronic sickness, or the debilities of extreme old age without feeling the burden of any moral claims on you. This philosophy ranks individual interests, in both earning and spending, above the interests of others.

Succeeding "across the board," then, may fall far short of joyous and productive living. Suppose I have potential in the five categories mentioned above: I'm a natural businessman (finance), I'm well-informed (information), I know how to organize others (relationships), I have abundant creativity (spirit), and stamina (time/energy). I could reach the outer limits of my potential in all the FIRST categories, and in so doing become a monster: monied, resourceful, manipulative, strong, and pigheaded.

Monster? Surely these five words describe the kind of characters who led the race to fortune in prewar America. Am I not being too hard on them? And yet it's surely significant that many of these same men felt their colossal achievements as a deadweight on their consciences, as a result of which, having heaped up their millions, they turned their attention from the exhausting struggle of making money to the happier business of distributing it.

John D. Rockefeller retired from Standard Oil in the 1890s and from then on devoted most of his time to benevolence. Andrew Carnegie began his campaign of charitable donation in the 1890s and by his death in 1918 had given away 90 percent of his fortune. Many others, including Wall Street speculator Bernard Baruch (during

World War One) and banker W.A. Harriman (in the 1930s), gave up commerce and went permanently into public service. Texas multimillionaire Hugh Roy Cullen summed up the switch in attitude neatly when he said: "I have taught my children that if they feel like buying some jewelry, they should find out how much it costs and then go out and give that amount to a school or hospital."

It's a credit to Paul Meyer, incidentally, that he didn't wait until he was superrich — and bored! — to ascend to the rarefied atmosphere of true philanthropy. He started at the age of 27 by giving 10 percent of his income. Since then he's increased the percentage of gross income he gives away each single year. He does it regardless of his financial situation.

So let me amend the definition of success. Because success has a moral edge. It means not just *approaching the outer limits of your potential in every area,* but *approaching the outer limits of your potential for good in every area.*

The addition of those two small words turns a Cinders into a Cinderella, a pumpkin into a carriage-and-four. We too often think of success as a quality an individual can possess in isolation. But success is not an individualistic concept. It is far more profoundly a community concept. We succeed over others: in a competitive society, that is inevitable and proper. But also, and more importantly, we succeed *with* them.

In a story a man visits both heaven and hell. They turn out to be much the same, both housing long tables where the dead sit down to enjoy a sumptuous eternal feast with the aid of three-foot-long silver spoons. The difference? In hell the guests try frantically and unsuccessfully to feed themselves, in heaven they have learned to feed one another.

Of course you don't have to visit the Other Side to see the importance of mutual giving. We quickly identify and shun those individuals who relate to us only for what they can get. To say somebody is "egotistical," "demanding," or "interested in no one but himself" says, in effect, that he concentrates obsessively on returns, on what he can get and not what he can give. We only spend time with him under duress. True, we all share the trait of self-centeredness. (In a group photo, who's the first one you look for?) But this more or less universal need to be loved and affirmed will never find satisfaction by thinking only of returns. It requires commitment to giving, a concerted and ongoing determination to serve one's own interests not directly, but indirectly by contributing to the well-being of the community.

Apply such thinking to finance and you will begin to see why the heroic philanthropists of a century ago made their money-making machines into alchemic engines converting raw currency into benevolence.[11] In his essay *Gospel of Wealth*, published in 1901, Andrew Carnegie foresaw rich and poor united under "a reign of harmony in which the surplus wealth of the few will become, in the best sense, the property of the many, because administered for the common good."[12]   Forty years later, the philanthropist Marshall Field III was arguing that wealth "carries with it certain obligations as a kind of payment for the privilege.   Those who neglect the obligations, I am convinced, speed the day when this privilege will be curtailed or perhaps denied."[13]

A cynic would call this making a virtue of necessity. The social upheavals of the early twentieth century taught the ruling classes that power can be overthrown. That being the case, a man owning a conspicuously large share of his country's wealth might see philanthropy as a means of self-preservation. Better to give away some than have all taken.

But if we take Field's comment at face value, the word "obligation" gives investment strongly moral overtones. In a world where so many are in so much need, it simply cannot be just for a single individual to use even innocently earned wealth purely for his or her own benefit. Carnegie again:

> This, then, is held to be the duty of the man of Wealth: First, to set an example of modest, unostentatious living, shunning display or extravagance; to provide moderately for the legitimate wants of those dependent upon him; and after doing so to consider all surplus revenues which come to him simply as trust funds, which he is called upon to administer, and strictly bound as a matter of duty to administer in the manner which, in his judgement, is best calculated to produce the most beneficial results for the community. . . .

The sentiment expressed here — perhaps more solidly a nineteenth century sentiment than a modern one — would have been shared by the other great philanthropists of Carnegie's generation — John D. Rockefeller, Henry Ford, and Marshall Field. All of them repeatedly described their property in terms of "trust," "tenure," "privilege," "duty," and "responsibility." They saw themselves (a little flatteringly, perhaps) as supremely gifted individuals, duty-bound by their success to bring, in Carnegie's words, their "superior wisdom, experience, and ability," to the service of their "poorer brethren. . .doing for them better than they would or could do for themselves."

There are notes of condescension and conceit in this which jar on modern ears. Nevertheless, the idea of the wealthy person as a trustee, not an owner, of wealth has important implications. Not only does investment serve our own interests, it is also *right.* The "success" of the wealthy is measured not in the breadth of the gully separating them from their less fortunate fellows, but in their determination to throw bridges across, recycling money to the society on which their financial wealth is built.

This idea of stewardship, of course, is basic to Paul Meyer's understanding of giving. Paul has surrendered his entire fortune to the glory of God and the benefit of mankind. His generosity knows no boundaries. Thank God for the philanthropy of all the celebrated personages I've referred to in this chapter. Yet it has to be said that in many cases their perceived "community" found limits at America's borders. Not so Paul Meyer.

Paul got rice to starving Ethiopians when none of the supplies sent by governments and aid agencies got past the leaders of the Addis Ababa government. He gives anonymously to help literally millions he'll never see in nations he may never visit. I know of multitudes in more than 145 nations who have benefitted — and continue to benefit — from his dynamic philanthropy. Paul Meyer's community spans the globe. And in freely embracing the whole of mankind, he himself finds wholeness.

4

THE RESOURCEFUL GIVER

I 've watched Paul Meyer create, acquire, and utilize resources. Observing him and replicating his example has enabled me to rise to a higher level of productivity than I would have dreamed possible.

Too many think in terms of "scarcity," of "lack"; Paul thinks in terms of abundance — and acts accordingly.

Let me "flesh out" the important component of positively exploiting resources in the abundant, giving lifestyle Paul employs — a lifestyle open to you as well.

Some years ago I attended the Southern Baptist Convention Pastor's Conference in Miami. It was the afternoon session of the first day. Few people came to that session, preferring to linger over lunch with colleagues they hadn't seen for a year. Most of those who did come, came late.

Ramsey Pollard, the president, said, "I now announce the recommendations for the coming year's nominating committee. They will select the officers for next year's pastor's conference." He called out one name after the other, and said, "Are you here?" Silence.

I was number seven. He said, "John Haggai." I said, "Here." The audience laughed and clapped.

Since nobody else on the list had turned up, they made me chairman of the committee even though I was only 31 years old. The outgoing chairman and new president, Dr. Sterling Price, felt I should be given a place on the next year's program, with the result that in Kansas City the following year I spoke to 10,000 church leaders. That first session on a Monday night, scheduled for 7 o'clock, normally attracted the smallest crowd of the evening although the press was there in force. That year, however, circumstances I've never understood delayed the call to order. I finally spoke just before 8:30. The press, understandably annoyed over the 90-minute wait, sat through my address — and many of them left immediately afterwards to turn in the story. They reported the address accurately and favorably. The next morning the front page of every major daily in America, from *New York Times* to *Los Angeles Examiner,* carried a substantive precis of my speech.

I know politicians who would kill for coverage like that — or at least who would pay through the nose to get it. I paid nothing at all. What did I invest? Answer: five minutes on a Monday afternoon the previous year, when I'd turned up and six other more senior people hadn't. That's as close to "something for nothing" as you're likely to see.

The incident tells us something about resources. I define resources as items you personally own, possess, have access to, or have discretion in deploying, and which constitute the sum total of your ability to achieve returns. I referred to one of them just now, by talking about my use of time. But altogether they number five: Finance, Information, Relationship, Spirit, and Time/energy — F,I,R,S,T, the FIRST resources.

1. Learn to use the FIRST resources

The two resources we think about most are the ones we can most easily measure: finance and time/energy.

When you buy a car you will usually ponder what kind of car you can *afford* — that is, you will assess the returns open to you in terms of the respective demands they make on your *financial* resources **(F)**. You have $8,000 in the bank; therefore, (leaving aside for the moment complications like credit agreements) you can afford an $8,000 car.

Your second measurable resource is time/energy **(T)**. We call this time/energy, not just energy or health, because for all practical purposes, time measures the amount of energy or attention you devote to any particular activity. When we say we have only 24 hours in a day, we acknowledge that our time/energy resources are limited. Again leaving aside complications, I can study for an exam this afternoon, or I can go out and play football — but I can't do both.

In addition, we possess three other, less easily quantified resources — information **(I)**, relationships **(R)**, and spirit **(S)**. Job

Even riding his bike, Paul never loses touch with business.

prospects depend substantially on experience, skill, and qualification — all of them informational qualities. We consider it an asset to be well-informed. We also consider it an asset to be well-connected, by which we mean that we have good relationships with people in influential positions — people we can rely on to help out if we need them. "Friends in high places" may help us get around awkward delays. Other friends may help us with simpler things, like managing children or stripping wallpaper. In addition, we place a high value on spiritual achievement, by which we might mean honesty, a talent for the violin, or a pleasant manner.

You sometimes hear it said of a wealthy person, "He doesn't know what he's worth." Given the constant fluctuation in the value of holdings — equities and real estate, for instance — that's usually true. However, Paul Meyer comes the closest of any man I've met to knowing his own financial condition. Almost every day, either in person or by phone and fax, he's in touch with his accountants.

And what's true of Paul's finances is true also of his other FIRST resources. His meticulously organized library, cassettes, and ephemeral articles underscore his attention to his information reserves. How many people do you know who maintain contact with classmates and teachers from his grammar school and high school? Paul does. He is a master at nurturing relationships. In terms of the spiritual and the mental, Paul spends a portion of each day in Bible study and prayer, finds time for two Bible studies a week, and faithfully attends church. Ask Paul where his Lear 55 will be on a particular day six months from now, and he'll whip out his pocket calendar and tell you not only where it will be but to what company that day's flights will be charged. He keeps tabs on time/energy expenditure. Believe me, Paul J. Meyer understands the use of FIRST resources.

When we start to include the FIRST resources in our thinking, the INVESTMENT ⇨ RETURN building block introduced in Chapter Two turns out to have three stages:

$$\text{RESOURCES} \Rightarrow \text{INVESTMENT} \Rightarrow \text{RETURN}$$

or,

$$\textbf{FIRST} \Rightarrow \text{INVESTMENT} \Rightarrow \text{RETURN}$$

We often think of resource planning as an exercise in cake-cutting: we can divide it up as we like, but in the end we have only so much cake to apportion. For instance, a person has a certain number of waking hours **(T)** available in the next month, and also has a certain projected income **(F)**. With a bit of good sense, both these can be budgeted in advance to make sure the person has enough money and time to do all the things he or she wants to do. Budgeting like this is much more efficient (and gives you far more control) than waiting till the end of each month to discover how much money you have left, or waiting till the end of each day to discover how much time you have left.

Of course, so long as you regard resources as being in fixed supply, like so much grain in a silo which can be conserved or paid out, costing soon comes down to simple arithmetic. You ask "Do I have enough money?" or "Can I spare the time?" If you don't have enough money or time, you must prioritize. You can't make your "cake" any bigger.

What you *can* do, however, is trade one resource for another. People seldom realize how easy this is — or how effective. For example:

$$\text{INVESTMENT} \Rightarrow \text{RETURN}$$

Time/energy   ⇨ Money
Employment   ⇨ Income

And the same is true in reverse. Thus:

INVESTMENT	⇨	RETURN
Money	⇨	Time/energy
Paying wages	⇨	Extra person-hours

Every one of the five resources is linked, in both directions, to every other. In some way each can be traded against the others, as illustrated in *Figure 4.1*.

Time/energy and money trade so easily that we rarely pause to think about it. Anyone in employment routinely exchanges time/energy for money. Every friendship or acquaintance cultivated denotes an exchange of time/energy for relationship. Every hour spent studying to gain a qualification or increase knowledge represents an exchange of time/energy for information.

We trade them in the opposite direction, too. We exchange money for time every evening we employ a baby sitter, for example. And on the same principle, a business leader like Paul Meyer "creates time" by paying employees to manufacture, pack, sell, and deliver his product. Similarly, the fact that you can exchange money for information is demonstrated daily, by the fee-paying student, the

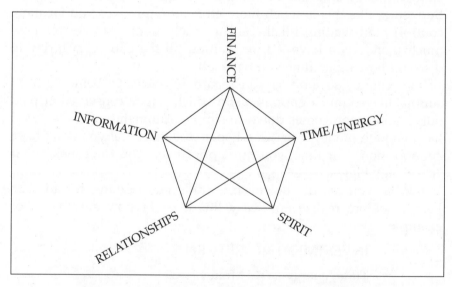

Figure 4.1: The pattern of FIRST resource exchanges.

book-buying reader, or by the story-hunting newspaper journalist. The role of money in creating relationships appears less obvious. We often repeat the old maxim that "money can't buy you love." True. It can't. Yet it can provide access to clubs or exclusive social circles through which valuable contacts can be made.

Such contacts are deemed valuable because they exchange into finance. In fact, we repeat another maxim here: that which matters in life isn't what you know, but who you know. And contacts don't just make you money. Relationships also open the gate to time/energy and information. We know that political power (a quality of relationship) brings influence, and that friends will often volunteer their help and give valuable advice. Paul Meyer, for example, once invited five young executives and their wives to be his special guests in Texas — to discuss stewardship and setting goals. That in itself was remarkable, given Paul's demanding schedule. What's more remarkable is the fact that he continues to maintain contact with them. In one instance, he sent materials every two weeks to fortify one of the young men, who said he was weak in a certain area of business.

Information, then, is itself a valuable resource. *What* we know to a large extent determines what kind of job we can hold down (and thus how much money we make). Information also exchanges with relationships (ask anyone who's married through a dating agency), and with time/energy whenever we use knowledge to cut out unnecessary work and thus "free up" time to do other, more productive tasks. Here, too, Paul Meyer excels, frequently sending staff on research assignments and targeting the acknowledged expert for information that will assist him in making effective decisions.

Finally, spirit. Of all the resources, spirit seems the least easy to exchange. Nevertheless, as anyone who has studied piano will know, time and money contribute to the development of musical creativity, as does a good relationship with the piano tutor. And while we don't "buy" spirituality in any commercial sense, we nevertheless invest time and money in quiet times and retreats, and see a concurrent growth of inner strength and of informational resources such as a deepening knowledge of Scripture.

As you will have noticed by now, the FIRST life-areas and the FIRST resources exactly mirror one another. When I succeed in the financial area of my life, my financial resources increase. When I make a new friend, my relationship resources increase. And so on.

Life can be seen as a process of exchanging FIRST resources, of building up resource "capital." We trade something which we have in surplus for something we lack but greatly value. In that sense, these resource exchanges resemble currency speculation. The information you gain from a contact may be of far greater use to you than the time/energy you invest in befriending him. You may get a better kept backyard by employing a professional gardener (exchanging money for time/energy) than by going out every Saturday afternoon and digging the flower beds yourself. And — just as with speculation — you will want to get maximum yield from your investment. That's why Paul Meyer did not formally finish college. After a few weeks, he met with the Dean. He told the Dean that the classes were moving too slowly. He then asked for a list of all the books required for the four years of classes. He said "I am disciplined, and I will finish this faster than four years." He did. And he's never stopped studying. The Ph.D.s who work for him envy both the breadth and depth of his knowledge.

Resource exchange is fundamental to philanthropy. True, you can give your resources directly. That's what happens when a student who loves children trains to be a teacher, or when an agricultural engineer concerned with world hunger offers his services to UNICEF. Often, though, philanthropic goals require specific skills or experience the philanthropist does not possess. And then resource exchanges come into play. The philanthropist can build up the resource he, or she, generates most efficiently — that is, finance — and then transform that finance into somebody else's time/energy.

Finally in this chapter, let's look at the building of two key FIRST resources: money and relationships.

2. Building relationships: the investment of influence

After World War II, the government kept tight price controls on automobiles. The demand for new cars exceeded the supply, and consequently some less scrupulous auto dealers began to avoid the price ceilings by accepting money under the table.

I had placed my order for a Chevrolet with my local dealership. I was number 7 on the list. Three days later, I was number 123. It didn't require the brains of a rocket scientist to know what had happened.

So I went over to Foster and Burns Nash Sales and Service in Spartanburg, South Carolina, and bought a Nash. The Nash wasn't as well known as the Chevrolet, but this Nash pleased me. In fact, I was so pleased, I influenced 16 people to purchase Nash automobiles from Foster and Burns. Foster and Burns wanted me to join them as a part-time salesman.

That's how relationships operate as a resource. Sixteen people trusted my judgment enough that they bought a Nash. Almost by definition a relationship is a long-term resource, for trust and confidence do not take root quickly. You have to nurture relationships, let them grow.

My assistant pastor at a church once said, "You speak much more firmly to me than you do to some of the lower-paid staff."

I said, "Yes, because I know you can handle it. I consider you to be on my level and, therefore, I have no hesitation in expressing concern when I feel you have not performed up to your capability. However, it would be unfair for me to speak in the same way to those who are in a clerical position, for instance." He referred to the almost patrician treatment I gave to my church organist. I said, "The organist does not have the opportunity of defending himself that you do. The very fact that I would express displeasure would overpower him, and I'm not going to do that."

Incidentally, to this day, the organist never comes through Atlanta without calling my house. While, as a young fellow, modesty prevented his "selling for what he was worth," today he has become a leader in his own right and has earned the respect both of his fellow musicians and of the multiplied tens of thousands who have heard him play.

The right handling of relationships might be termed an "investment of influence." I borrow the phrase from the title of a book published in 1903 by Newell Dwight Hillis. Hillis defines the "investment of influence" in a particularly striking fashion:

> The charioteer holds the reins, guides his steeds, restrains or lifts the scourge. Similarly man holds the reins of influence over man, and is himself in turn guided. So friend shapes and molds friend. This is what gives its meaning to conversation, oratory, journalism, reforms. Each man stands at the center of a great network of voluntary influence for good.

Men or women, wealthy or poor, literate or illiterate, famous or obscure, we all wield influence over others. We do so whether we know it or not. We cannot help it. And if we are wise, Hillis says, we will *invest* that influence as we would invest money in stocks or bonds or real estate, to exploit to the fullest its potential for accomplishing good.

Investing influence goes beyond networking. We use the term networking to describe the establishing of relationships for the purpose of achieving predetermined goals. Networking can achieve great results — humanitarian, political, business, educational, professional, even spiritual. But members of a network won't always become friends. In most instances, people you network with do not maintain a continuing relationship with you after the objective has been achieved. Networking doesn't require you to care for people, or for them to care for you.

True, out of a network can come lasting friendships, but that's not the purpose of the network. A networker need not invest compassion, heart, soul, unlimited time. He or she need feel no personal responsibility for other individuals in the network. The alliance creates, so to speak, a marriage of convenience. It requires no overarching focus of loyalty, no incentive to long-term commitment. The networker does not invest in the relationships; he merely uses them.

By contrast, investment implies the deliberate cultivation of friendship — something that demands far more attention than sending the occasional Christmas card. As Hillis pointed out, in a chapter called (rather disconcertingly to modern ears) "Helpfulness of the Higher Manhood," friendship possesses special power. "No one," he says,

> can resist its sweet solicitude. It undermines like a wave, it rends like an earthquake, it melts like a fire, it inspires like music, it binds like a chain, it detains like a good story, it cheers like a sunbeam. No other power is immeasurable. For things have only partial influence over living men. Forests, fields, skies, tools, occupations, industries—these all stop in the outer court of the soul. It is given to affection alone to enter the sacred inner precincts.

Friendship establishes contact, trust, and reciprocity. "Give abundant thought to wires and cables and buttresses," writes Hillis, "and nature will give the bridge across the Firth of Forth."

Paul Meyer has no trouble building influence on friendship. He recalls an after-dinner conversation with one particularly wealthy friend.

"Marty, I want to ask you a question," said Paul.

Marty replied, "Go ahead."

"If you died tonight, what would your property be worth?"

"$300,000,000," Marty said.

Paul cast a glance over his shoulder. "There's nobody listening," he said. "How much have you given? What's the biggest thing you've ever done?"

Marty hesitated.

Paul pressed him. "You could give away 100 million and not miss it."

Marty said, "Well, I still owe 50 million. . ."

"What's that got to do with it?" Paul demanded. "Why don't you give them the stock? The best way not to pay an estate tax is to not have an estate, get rid of it. You can give it away and it won't cost you anything. It won't cost anybody anything." He dropped his voice. "So what's the big gift?"

Marty said, "I gave a big gift to the university."

"How much?"

Marty named the figure and Paul laughed out loud. "That's a joke. You say they made you, that you owe everything to them. I think you cheated them. Why don't you give them ten million? What's ten million bucks to you?"

"I could square off with him," Paul recalls," and I think from that evening on he really liked me. I told him that I'm not going to wait until I die. I'm not going to leave an estate, I'm going to give it away. I'm giving it away as fast as I can make it, and faster."

Marty began to think and give in dimensions totally foreign to him prior to his friendship with Paul.

Investing influence, then, will move you to analyze the way you handle your relationships. And of course that goes far beyond contacts in the business and professional worlds.

"One of the groups of people I want to influence," says Paul Meyer, "is my children. Every once in awhile I'll just have a meeting with them, or I'll write them a letter or a memo or something, and tell them this is what it is all about. I remember writing to Larry one

Paul with his children. Left to right: Billy, Janna, Paul, Leslie, Larry and Jim. "I'd like our family to do more for Christ than any family I've ever met. I have to be a role-model to get that done."

time, and I said, 'In your pursuit of chasing the long green and climbing Mount Everest, be sure that you do it for the right reasons and your priorities stay straight.' I've discussed with my children those right priorities over and over and over and over again."

Supremely, Paul wants to make sure every member of his family knows Jesus Christ and finds salvation: children, grandchildren, and spouses.

"I want to make sure our whole family ministers. I'd like our family to do more for Christ than any family I've every met. I have to be a role model to get that done. I tell them every time I see them. I told little Adam, Billy's son, 'God made you something special. I don't know where He's going to use you but he's going to use you some place dynamic.' I think every time I say that it penetrates his mind. And even Jim's oldest son, Mike. I said to him, 'Mike, I guess in one way you can say I'm a lousy grandfather because I don't do a lot of things grandfathers do, and I treat you more like an adult than a child. I have always treated people that way. What I really would like to be, along with your dad, is a spiritual influence on you.' Mike doesn't talk much, but he said, 'You are.' He's six-foot-three, and a good looking guy.   He goes to Texas A & M University and is studying business. He gets excellent grades. I would like to be an influence on him."

3. Building finance: the art of saving

Oddly, people neglect one of the most profitable and important exchanges between time/energy and finance. I mean *saving*.

Paul Meyer grasped the importance of saving early on.

"I made a nickel working all day at age six. My father drove me to the end of Shelley Avenue off White Creek Road and let me out of the car to pick prunes with migrant farm workers. I picked one lug-box during the day and earned a nickel. I probably still have it."

Paul gave himself to the job with characteristic vigor, and a few years later set out to break the world record.

"I got up at 2 a.m., hung flashlights in the trees, and worked till late in the evening. I was wrung out. But I made 25 cents a box, so I earned $25.25 — approximately the same amount that men earned per week at that time. I was higher than a kite. I told my dad about it. He was reading the paper. He pulled the paper down, looked me in the eye and said, 'Don't tell me how much you earned today. Show me how much of it you will have five years from now, and I'll tell you how much you earned today.'"

The boy went to his room angry. But the incident imprinted on his mind a vital idea. Earning, he realized, was only the first step in maximizing money as a resource.

"I had thrifty parents as role models, who did not believe in debt. I have been a rat-holer, a sandbagger, and a saver all my life — the dollar amount I have never said. The percentage is at least 10 percent plus since age twelve — every paycheck since that day for 52 years." He smiles. "If I look you in the eye and tell you I am broke, I am lying because rat-holed some place is a nest egg to start again."

Look at Paul's personal development program on building financial success, and you find this experience codified as a principle he calls The Tenth Multiple.

"Too many people — especially those living on a fixed income — never think to pay themselves first. They are so conditioned by attractive advertising and easy credit that they spend their incomes on status symbols which actually have little real value. They pay the butcher, the baker, and the candlestick maker first; then, if there is anything left over, they pay themselves. Too often, nothing is left."

Paul isn't ashamed to labor the point. "You never, never, never pay the people you owe first and pay what is left over to charity or to yourself. I do not know in my lifetime of anyone who has succeeded in saving a great deal of money by investing only the surplus. Emerson said, 'If you cannot save money, the seed of success is not in you.'"

Meantime Paul Meyer proofs his saving against fluctuations in the market by keeping his financial eggs in as many baskets as he can find. You could nickname him, "Mr. Diversification."

"I spread my risk in that I make money more ways than anybody could imagine," he explains. "The public's perception of me is that I make it from the Success Motivation Institute. If you ask anybody in this town, 'What does Paul Meyer do?' nine out of ten will say 'SMI.' Me? I just smile. The motivation business is our core business. But SMI doesn't represent two percent of my assets or income. I spread it out, spread it out, spread it out, and spread it out."

Mastering resources, then, demands a long-term perspective on resource planning. Any particular return can be achieved by costing the project in money and time/energy, and then seeing how many projects you have available money and time/energy to complete. At the very least that produces increased efficiency.

But the real art lies in exchanging your resources skillfully enough to maximize them — to multiply and deepen your relationships, to add constantly to your knowledge and expertise, to eliminate unnecessary activities and free up time/energy, and, most important, to increase your financial power.

5

THE GIVER WHO DREAMS BIG

E very child has a dream.
   When Paul Meyer was a Boy Scout, he had a dream to be an Eagle Scout. His brother Carl, who was three years older, had become the first Eagle Scout in Troop 34. Paul could hardly wait for his twelfth birthday to arrive. He'd already mastered the information to achieve the Tenderfoot and Second Class. His progression to become the troop's second Eagle Scout marked his first — and formative — experience in goal-setting. He looks back on this experience as the foundation stone of his entire business career.

But return to the beginning: the dream. Because it's the dream

Paul as a boy scout. His drive to become his troop's second Eagle Scout marked a formative experience in goal-setting.

that drives everything else. It's the dream that motivates. And dreams should dominate financial giving.

For example, think of the last time you made a donation.

Very likely you made it because someone asked you to. You received a mailing, and you sent back $30 with no intention of giving to that cause on a regular basis. You felt you had discharged your responsibility. And yet if that cause deserves one gift, why not several and periodic gifts? Most not-for- profit organizations would function much more productively if they knew in advance when and how much money donors planned to give. Or does the donor consider that cause not so worthy after all?

Too often our giving is haphazard. Too often we regard giving simply as an end in itself, as though we had to meet some sort of quota. Once the quota's filled, we feel the glowing satisfaction of a duty discharged and put away our checkbooks. I do not disparage the placing of limits on generosity: it is no small matter regularly to tithe — and even give above the tithe. But to derive the full benefits from giving, you need a strong sense of purpose. You need to know *why* you're giving. You need to begin with the dream.

1. Dream bigger — and bigger

You can dream about anything — the kind of person you might be, the kind of things you might do, the kind of money you might earn. And, if you want to know in detail how to turn the energy of your dreams into motivation, I refer you to the master of motivation, Paul J. Meyer. Nowhere will you find a more powerful, more comprehensive, more incisive instruction in the use of dreams than in Paul's materials. I keep them constantly at hand — on my desk, in fact. I stand in awe of them. I wholeheartedly recommend them.

My concern in this discussion, however, focuses not on dreaming in general, but on dreaming for giving. What follows is thoroughly consistent, indeed, draws its inspiration from Paul J. Meyer's material. But it looks at dreams from a particular angle, with a particular goal in mind: becoming an effective and prolific giver.

So, what does the giver need to know first about dreams? Simply this: don't suffocate them. Too often as adults we put up an electric fence to separate our dreams from our real lives, and consequently, even if we dream a lot, we seldom see our dreams as relevant to the workaday world. We dream for solace, not for inspiration. Our dreams begin, "If only. . . ." Also we often dream in a sporadic and disorganized manner. Dreams come and go. We fail to hold onto them. We don't act on them.

I've heard Paul say many times, "Most people start turning off their dream machine at about age nine. They hear such demotivators as: 'You ask too many questions. Don't be so inquisitive. When you grow up you'll understand. Stop bothering me. That can't work. Others have tried it and failed.' Turn your dream machine back on." Paul sees possibilities and potentialities the average person never sees. He relates the normally unrelated. He thinks outside the box. Dreams make this type of creative thinking possible.

Dreaming, then, contains enormous creative potential. It provides a window into our hearts, telling us what really matters to us, what we really desire. We should treat our dreams with respect. In saying "I have a dream," as Martin Luther King once did, you do not necessarily name an unattainable wish: you turn a wish into a direction, a dream into a plan.

Nehemiah turned his dream into a plan when he turned his sorrow over the destruction of Jerusalem into a positive agenda to restore the city walls. Making that transition isn't easy. It demands two things. One, suspending the critical faculty that says to each dream "That's impossible — forget it!" And two, taking dreams seriously enough to write them down. Get yourself a quiet place, some undisturbed time, and subject your dreams to the discipline of method.

You may define a dream a desired return. You can write it down, define it, sharpen it, and translate it into specific actions. But to do that, you have to know what your dreams are, and how they connect to your "real" life. How much of your daily life, for example, do your dreams really cover? When we commend the "balanced life," we mean that one category never receives so much of our energy and attention that others fall into neglect. Ponder again the five resources — the five life-areas — we looked at earlier:

FINANCE	Income
	Financial investments
	Debts
	Philanthropy

INFORMATION	Qualifications
	Learning
	Reading/study/media awareness
	Work skills
RELATIONSHIPS	Family
	Friends
	Colleagues
	Distant or occasional relationships
SPIRIT	Worship
	Values
	Creativity
	Restorative experience and
	personal ambition
TIME/ENERGY	Physical fitness
	Mental fitness
	Stress control
	Diet

Reflect on your dreams. How are they distributed within this fivefold division? Are there any blank spaces? If so, what dreams would you fill them with? Most important, are those dreams for yourself, or for others?

That last question's a clincher. If you want to be a giver, you have to give yourself room to think of others. But how?

Here's my suggestion, an adaptation of what I've observed in Paul, and which I've found helpful. When you have gathered your thoughts, write them down on a chart like the one in *Figure 5.1*. Appendix 1 at the back of this book contains five similar charts — one for each resource area. Use the left column to set out your dreams. Remember, all you are doing here is brainstorming. Don't allow any inhibition to thwart you. What matters isn't that you can see a way to realizing a dream, but that the dream truly belongs to you. If you want a classic car, write that down. If you want to open a retreat for the homeless, or support a children's charity, write that down. If you want to ride through Nepal on a yak, write that down,

TYPE OF RETURN:	BENEFITS TO ME:	BENEFITS TO OTHERS:
RANK ( )		
RANK ( )		
RANK ( )		
RANK ( )		
RANK ( )		

Figure 5.1: Dreams and benefits

too. Don't worry if it sounds foolish, idealistic, naive, vague, or selfish, provided that it honestly expresses your desire. At this stage you don't need to assess your dreams, or attempt to rank them in order of importance. Just get them out of your head and on to paper. I've never seen Paul without something to write on and write with — even when he's on the beach.

Once you've put down everything that you can think of in the first column — and that may take you some time — turn to columns 2 and 3. Sit back, look at your lists, and ask yourself, "Why is that a desirable return? What benefits would it bring, once achieved?"

It's essential to think clearly here, because the benefits are, in a sense, the "goals beyond the goals," the final returns to which your wishes are themselves investments. You should think carefully, then, whether a certain return will give you what you want. Why *do* you want to raise your annual income by, say, $10,000? What, specifically, is the *advantage* in attaining a certain college degree? Really you are exploring motives, and making sure that the return you've named in any particular area is, for you personally, worth having. And notice something important. Even your own personal goals will have benefits for others. Make sure you think these out. Write down how the goals you set for your own benefit give something to others too.

Using the second column on the chart, then, you might start your entry like this:

PHYSICAL RETURN:	BENEFITS TO ME:	BENEFITS TO OTHERS:
RANK ( ) Become a strong swimmer	1. Enjoyment 2. Greater physical fitness	

But what benefits will you bring to others? Plenty. Because regular exercise improves your general state of health and your projected longevity, it will also increase your ability to care for your family as homemaker and/or provider. It also becomes another interest to be shared with others. So in the end the chart begins to fill up something like this:

PHYSICAL RETURN:	BENEFITS TO ME:	BENEFITS TO OTHERS:
RANK ( ) Become a strong swimmer	1. Enjoyment 2. Greater physical fitness	1. Fitness means security for family 2. An activity to share with my wife

Now let me give you a challenge.

Go through that same exercise again, but this time try to find a dream that will benefit another person *first*. In other words, name your objective, and then move straight to column three. Supporting relief aid, for example, has the explicit aim of benefiting others:

FINANCIAL RETURN:	BENEFITS TO ME:	BENEFITS TO OTHERS:
Give $100/month to overseas aid		Prevent starvation

Your generosity saves lives. But it benefits you as well. You gain a sense of fulfillment and self-esteem; you deepen your understanding of an important global issue; and you feel a stronger bond with those less fortunate than yourself. You may wish to remind yourself also that giving carries its own built in fail-safe protection — since over the long haul your investment in charitable concerns will bear real fruit for you. Perhaps your completed entry will look like this:

FINANCIAL RETURN:	BENEFITS TO ME:	BENEFITS TO OTHERS:
Give $100/month to famine relief	1. I feel I am helping to alleviate suffering 2. I learn about the places where the charity works 3. I don't lose out financially	Prevent starvation

Remember that writing down your dreams in this way creates a synergy of the senses. It creates sensory-rich impressions on the brain. It programs the right brain even as the words program the left brain. It stimulates the visual: you see the words and visualize their meaning. It brings into play the tactile sense as you feel the writing instrument or the keys on the computer. It brings into play the olfactory sense: you can almost smell the ink of the pen, the identifying smell of the pad, or the ozone of the computer. It brings into play the kinesthetic factor as your arm and hand move.

2. Put second things second

You can earn a living in many ways — but you can do only so many jobs.

You may accumulate many experiences — but you have only so many years to live.

You may give to many good causes — but you can generate only so much time and money.

You are finite. You have to make choices. You have to prioritize. But the most common form of prioritization is misdirected. Such are the demands of the modern workplace that many professional men and women earn their promotions only by ruthlessly preferring their careers over their other life-areas. Top male executives often become absentee husbands. They never find the balance; extra investment in their careers can only be found by depriving wives and children. It's a painfully familiar dilemma which more and more people now try to resolve in favor of their families.

We need to prioritize, then, not *among* life-areas (that only leads

Jane and Paul with a member of the H.I. faculty, international leadership guru Fr. Anthony D'Souza. Paul says he supports Haggai Institute because "I like to get as much bang for the buck as I can."

to imbalance), but *within* them.

"I don't know when I reached this decision," a friend told me recently, "but a few years ago I decided I could not give to lots of ministries in a significant way. So I really have five major ministries to which I'm giving money. And then I will give small amounts occasionally to other people and to specific organizations. My view is that if you give a little bit to everybody, you really don't help anybody at all, and you really can't be supportive of the causes you really believe in."

In identifying "causes you really believe in," you are in effect naming a reason to choose one financial priority over another. As a side effect, you also cut down the number of potential beneficiaries, and make it easier to assess their respective merits. It's important, after all, to know not just that a charity provides, say, care for the mentally handicapped, but that the charity directs its efforts to those who most badly need its help.

Paul Meyer explains his support of Haggai Institute in bluntly commercial terms.

"You see, I like to get as much bang for the buck as I can. Traditional missionaries cost us a million dollars over a lifetime. They have culture shock when they get overseas; they take long breaks; and for the first five years they don't know whether they are on foot or horseback. And for that you are sending them $40,000 a year, all the time. But with Haggai Institute, it's a one-time pay. They recruit people indigenous to the culture, and train them in leadership and evangelism so they can stand on their own two feet. Instead of giving them fish, we give them a rod. So this is the number-one place that we give. It's far more effective — and trust me, I am pitched by everybody. Everything else pales compared to it. I can't find anything that even comes close."

There are parallels here between Paul Meyer and Andrew Carnegie, who argued that

> the best means of benefiting the community is to place within its reach the ladders upon which the aspiring can rise — parks, and means of recreation, by which men are helped in body and mind; works of art, certain to give pleasure and improve the public taste, and public institutions of various kinds, which will improve the general condition of the people; — in this manner returning their surplus wealth to the mass of their fellows in the forms best calculated to do them lasting good.[14]

The "lasting good" Carnegie achieved is attested by the presence of his barrel-chested bust in many a public library. But equally good reasons exist for giving only to low-profile organizations. Although Paul Meyer has given a large one-time donation to a great university on the strength of his many associations with it and its personnel, in general, he favors obscurer projects simply because they have not already attracted money from elsewhere.

By the same token, Paul prioritizes Christian work. In that, he differs from the mainstream of American society: from the wealthy political liberals who prefer to have the taxpayer underwrite their programs to assist the disadvantaged. And from the wealthy conservatives who missed the opportunity offered by Mr. Reagan's "volunteerism" in 1981, choosing instead to spend the benefits from their reduced taxes upon themselves.

Paul Meyer directs most of his philanthropy (in money and in time/energy) toward Christ-centered causes. He remarks that others will give to the zoos, the arts, the museums, the symphony, the historical sites, and the other secular institutions and charities. They will give little, if any, to Christ-centered organizations, and almost nothing to those enterprises spreading the message of Christ's redeeming love in foreign lands.

Yet Paul prioritizes Christian work because he understands its permanence. Others have seen the same thing. John D. Rockefeller and his son made substantial grants to Christian organizations, as did J. Howard Pew of the Sun Oil Company and the financier J. Pierpont Morgan. The late Cecil B. Day, founder of Days Inns; the late Guy W. Rutland (whom Paul dubs "a great inspiration to me"), who was majordomo of Motor Convoy; and the late Arnold Browning, hotel and property magnate focused on similar priorities. These stand in that small cadre we might dub the "exceptionals." They, like Paul, have thought and moved in the rarefied atmosphere of the eternal, the permanent. They are the too-few stalwart modern philanthropists who synchronize their priorities with the express command of God in Scripture, who march to the divine drumbeat. They impact the world — yes, the world — for God.

Were Paul Meyer to give the millions to secular organizations that he gives to the permanent betterment and eternal benefit of mankind, he would gain celebrity status. He does not seek it. He revels in his privacy. And he prioritizes the permanent. The Bible says, "The things which are seen are temporal; the things which are not seen are eternal." Paul invests in lives, the essence of which no one sees — only the expression of the essence. He values the eternal, with the full knowledge that it's an eternal orientation that makes the greatest contribution to the temporal good.

How do I know these things? Because I've had the high honor of seeing Paul's financial records, his prayer journal, and his affirmations — in addition to many of the results of his philanthropy.

Prioritization matters. In all five life-areas, then, you need to begin by ranking your dreams in order of importance. You will notice that all five charts in Appendix 1 carry ranking spaces. If you could only accomplish one return in each life-area, what would it be? Which is most important after that? Bear in mind, of course, that at this stage the ranking is provisional. You will have resources to achieve several returns in each life-area. Questions of "how many" and "which" will be settled only when you come to "cost" the options and work out how to combine them in a single life strategy.

3. From your dream forge a mission

Many of the things Paul Meyer needed to know about life he learned in his father's workshop.

One incident particularly sticks in Paul's mind. He was in the garage one day, hammering on an old bike. His father said, "Hold it, hold it. Take it apart the way the manufacturer put it together. There's an exact way it was assembled — Part A, Part B, Part C, and Part D. If it has twenty-six parts, you start with Z, and then Y, X, and go backwards. You can take it apart, put it together, take it apart, put it together."

So Paul carefully dismantled the bicycle, laying the pieces out one at a time. When he'd finished, his father pointed at the last piece and said, "Now start back here and put them back together." And when Paul had reassembled the bicycle the father said, "Do it again."

By the time he'd stripped and reassembled the bike twice, Paul Meyer knew a lot about bicycles. His father looked at the reconstructed bike and said, "Listen. You can do the same now with an automobile engine or an aircraft engine. You can do the same thing with your day. You'd better remember that all your life. Don't force things, don't force life, don't force change. If you have a problem, remember you've just taken a wrong turn in the road."

Transition? Dream planning begins with translating each dream into a mission: framing your final objective in such a way that you can see what investments must be used to accomplish it. In the case of putting a bike together, the return is self-evident — you want a bike you can ride. But most dreams need careful translation.

Say, for instance, you dream of being a "good tennis player." You could represent your ambition easily enough using the

INVESTMENT ⇨ RETURN diagram:

      INVESTMENT ⇨ RETURN

      ?   ⇨ Become good tennis player

No problem with motivation here. You can imagine yourself out on the court playing a strong, accurate serve and an attacking return. You warm to the sense of accomplishment that comes with mastering the sport. You know greater physical fitness will increase your life expectancy and so indirectly benefit your family. The idea excites you and motivates you: you're just itching to buy a racquet, get out there, and start playing.

On its own, however, the aim of being a "good tennis player" doesn't get you far. *How* good? How will you know if you've reached your goal or not? Over what period of time will you achieve this transformation? Clearly you need to give the phrase "good tennis player" a precise dollars-and-cents meaning. You need to rewrite the diagram, perhaps like this:

      INVESTMENT ⇨ RETURN

      ?   ⇨ Win my local club singles
                                   competition in three years' time.

Swallowing hard? If so, dream planning has begun to do its work, for the first requirement of a return — a goal or a mission — is that it be *specific*. By substituting a concrete value for that all-purpose word "good," you make it reflect clearly and unambiguously what you propose to do. At the same time, of course, it makes attainment measurable. Not only do you know where you are going; you also know how many miles you need to cover in order to get there. By its very nature, a return acts as a yardstick.

The second function of a return is to be *attainable*. All other things being equal, three years should be long enough to win you a local title. But *are* all other things equal? Check it out. If everyone else in the club is hopeless you may want to shorten your deadline or set your sights a little higher. Similarly, you can be overambitious: set out to become CEO of Chase Bank by the age of 23 and you're going to be disappointed. The art is to keep returns *within* your capacity, but *tough enough* to stretch you. That crucial difference is basic to Paul Meyer's philosophy. It separates the Apollo program, which eventuated in a man setting foot on the moon, from the Star Wars program, whose promise of a satellite-based antimissile laser system simply outstripped the technology.

Complex technical programs like Apollo, of course, remind us that an investment — represented as a "?" in the diagram above — itself usually breaks down into several smaller investment-return transactions. In the case of assembling a bicycle, this involves making smaller investments (in practice, bolting pieces on) in the right order. You can't, for instance, put the wheel on the bicycle until you've put the tire on the wheel. A has to go before B, and B before C. In other cases, like the one I quoted earlier about house-buying, a given return may require the simultaneous accomplishment of two or more investments. Regularly spending Saturday afternoon with the children necessitates two investments, neither of which is dependent on the other, but both of which are indispensable to produce the desired result:

INVESTMENT ⇨ RETURN

Create time in
my schedule
                        Spend 2-5 pm
            ⇨   Saturday
Create time in   with the children
children's schedule

Usually these "intermediate returns" will emerge clearly if you ask yourself what obstacles separate you from your chosen objective. Go back to the tennis.

It may surprise you to know that Paul Meyer dreamed of playing tennis. He was forty-six. His objective? To become a ranked player for his age-group at the Texas state level. Since he'd never played tennis before, he used an array of intermediate goals to develop and perfect his game. Before he'd even lifted a racquet he placed on his desk an affirmation saying "I am a Class-A tennis player."

The methods he used actually to *become* a Class-A tennis player stagger the imagination. He regularly studied around 20 different videos of great tennis players. He took lessons from Rod Laver, the

*Paul playing tennis. Before he'd even lifted a racquet he placed
on his desk an affirmation saying "I am a Class-A tennis
player."*

world's number-one tennis player, from Roy Emerson, who'd won
more tournaments than anyone else at that time, and from Russell
Seymour, the top player in Paul's own age-group.

So he'd always have a court to play on (an important goal) he
bought a local tennis club, installing the number-one Texas player
Robert Trogolo as resident pro and subsequently sponsoring him for
a world tour. In all, Paul took 300 lessons, read 20 books, and went
to four different tennis camps. Long before such technology became
commonplace he bought a computerized ball machine (it came from
India), using its 7,000 shot-variations to simulate the style of targeted
opponents until he was good enough to beat them. (The technique
worked. After a month's practice with the machine Paul lashed a
particularly tough opponent, 6-1, 6-3.)

Another — and vital — intermediate goal involved installing a
practice court at his house. He couldn't build it on the grounds

*The winners. Paul and doubles partner Jim Curry
display their trophies.*

because he lacked the space, and anyway the property sloped down
to a lake. So he decided to put the court on stilts over the water. He
borrowed a line from the song "I'm gonna build me a mountain" to
create a new affirmation: "I'm gonna build me a tennis court." His
wife Jane thought the whole plan was bizarre.

Before he could put it into effect, however, a lady knocked on
his door and said, "I've heard about your goal. I have a house with
enough level ground for a tennis court, and I'd love to buy your
house by the lake. Can we make a deal?" Paul sold his house to her
immediately. The next day he bought hers.

Paul's progress in tennis has reached many high points. When
he was age 53, he and Robert Trogolo played the men's championship
together against America's top college players. They lost to the
number-one pair in Texas — but at one point had been serving for
the match. Paul wanted to prove that people any age could take up
anything — and win. Today, he still ranks among the top players of
his age group in Texas — a stunning achievement, since most of the

Dream planner

DREAM: Become a good tennis player
MISSION: Win local singles championship in 3 years

$	🕐	SECONDARY INVESTMENTS	PRIMARY INVESTMENTS
		1 hour in weight room 3 times per week. Progressive weight training	Fitness: Be able to lift 150 lbs. (70Kg) 30 times on bench press
		Run 10-30 minutes 5 times per week	Fitness: Be able to run for 30 minutes without fatigue
		4 hours of tennis lessons each week	Technique: Continue tennis lessons every week
		Watch video of professional tennis match once a week	
		4 matches per week. Select opponents according to skill level	Technique: Play and beat every other club member

Figure 5.2: A dream planner in progress

others have been playing since childhood.

But back to *your* plan. For starters you know that to win the singles title you'll need to be both fit and skilled — each a return following from previous investments. You might sketch out a plan like the one shown in *Figure 5.2*. This chart — which again owes much to the inspiration of Paul Meyer — I call a dream planner. It enables you to put investments in the right order. Notice that your mission — to win the local singles championship in three years — breaks down into smaller objectives, which break down further into the kinds of routine goals you can enter in your daily organizer.

This is sound psychology. Too often we allow our dreams to stay just that — dreams, unrealized and unfulfilled. We can see no way to attain them; they stand on the far side of a fast flowing river. In effect, the dream planner shows us the stepping stones across the current. Each one represents a small step, but taken together, and in the right sequence, they lead us from one side of the water to the other.

For that reason, perhaps, one of the immediate payoffs of dream planning is a strong sense of control. Knowing that you need to raise your annual income from $40,000 to $70,000 over the next two years may simply crush your resolve; but to have a concrete, realizable plan for making that transition happen will motivate you and boost your confidence.

And it's the same, only more so, with giving. Allocate even a small proportion of your income to specific charitable projects, and you will have the immense satisfaction of knowing you're a donor, a contributor, a focused and responsible person who not only *wishes* to improve society but actually *does* it.

What demands will realizing a dream make on your resources? Well, break it down on a dream planner and you can soon cost your tennis project in terms of projected outlays of money and time/energy, as in *Figure 5.3*. Suddenly your dream translates into the nuts-and-bolts language of budgeting and time-management.

Dream planning, of course, is a method of goal-setting — an art of which Paul Meyer has long been America's leading exponent. Paul can name between five and ten goals in each of his life-areas. But remember, the number of goals you have is secondary. What matters is learning to make your goal-setting *work*.

"It's almost spooky," Paul says. "It's a foregone conclusion if I

Dream planner

DREAM: Become a good tennis player
MISSION: Win local singles championship in 3 years

$	⏱	SECONDARY INVESTMENTS	PRIMARY INVESTMENTS
$200/yr	Tues+ Thu 8am-9	1 hour in weight room 2 times per week. Progressive weight training	Fitness: Be able to lift 150 lbs. (70Kg) 30 times on bench press
	M+F 8am-9	Run 10-30 minutes 2 times per week	Fitness: Be able to run for 30 minutes without fatigue
$500/yr	Sat 9 am-11	4 hours of tennis lessons each week	Technique: Continue tennis lessons every week
$5/mth	1st Sun 10pm-11	Watch video of professional tennis match once a week	
	Sat 9 am-11	4 matches per week. Select opponents according to skill level	Technique: Play and beat every other club member

Figure 5.3: A completed dream planner

(a) put it down as a goal; (b) list what obstacles and roadblocks stand between me and the goal; (c) list the ways around the obstacles, over them, or through them; (d) list what needs of mine will be met if I do it; and (e) list the action steps and the time it takes to achieve whatever goal I am after. When I do that, you can pretty much take it to the bank.

"It is a system that works if believed in, thought out, actionized, and applied."

A dream planned is a dream realized.

6

THE GIVING GOAL-SETTER

P aul Meyer's lawyer Mike Boreland once told him straight out, "Your theory of giving won't hold water."

Paul asked him to explain.

Boreland said, "What is your real goal?"

"Two things," Paul replied. "I want to make tens of millions. And I want to die broke."

Boreland shook his head. "You can't do it. No matter how much you give away — and you're unloading it like crazy off the back end — at night you dream up a new idea and start a new company and you're loading it on the front end."

Unwilling to concede the argument, Paul countered, "Okay. You tell me I'm earning faster than I give. I've only one question to ask you. How many pages was the will when I signed it last year?"

"Ninety pages," said Boreland.

"And my new one — how many pages?"

Boreland said, "Eighty-seven."

"So I win. I have less to give away now than I used to."

A lawyer's smile spread over Boreland's face. He said, "You're wrong. This year I put it in smaller print."

Part of Paul's genius lies in turning philanthropy itself into an entrepreneurial concern. His problem — if it is a problem — is not that he fails to reserve and cultivate funds from which to give, but that he often makes money faster than he had anticipated and has more to give than he had planned. This snowball effect, however, authenticates his philosophy and validates his approach. He wants his giving to enjoy the permanence factor. He strives for longevity as well as multiplication in his philanthropy. He yearns for his money to outlive him even though generosity leads him constantly to divest his estate.

Not only has he provided comprehensively in his will; more remarkably, in January of each year he takes out insurance on every pledge, to protect beneficiaries from a loss of expected income in the event of his death. I've met many impressive benefactors in my time, but I've never met one who covered his giving like that. Such is the genius of Paul J.Meyer.

1. Be proactive

In Paul's view, the donor should assume a more extensive role in his philanthropy than just the signing of checks. To secure optimum returns in philanthropy, financial investment must be undergirded with creative thinking. Paul has elevated this unique approach to a fine art.

He asks all the charities he supports to send him a wish list once a month.

"They aren't sharp enough to keep sending it to me. But needs are so easy to supply. Every time a request comes in, it'll hook somebody's mind and he'll say, 'Oh, I can get hold of one of those.' Like in one of our projects, we have two hundred children, and we teach them in the afternoon, tutor them. We bought an old building. I put a new tin roof on it. I put the computers in there and I bought all the school supplies. Students from Baylor do the tutoring.

"I go over there about once a month to meet the children and talk to them. We call it the Community Training Center. Last month I bought them a bus and told them that if any children did well we'd reward them by taking them over to the other side of town to the Boys and Girls Club. We try to use that as a catalyst. Over 2,000 children live in that area. It's a challenging social environment. We're trying to set up a Boys and Girls Club right in the middle of it."

Notice Paul's use of the pronoun "we"; he is involved in these enterprises. As often as not, he initiates them. His work with young people shows a constant flair for innovation.

"I got a group of young people nine years ago and I said, 'How would you like to meet with me once a month? I'll meet with you a hundred times, and I'll promise you those hundred meetings will change your lives forever. You will learn how to accept responsibility for your future. You will learn how to set and achieve goals, how to make decisions, how to have discernment about people by looking at them and meeting with them — and all of that through a Christian

Paul in Washington, D.C., with his Success Club. Through Paul's influence, the young people have seen the Judiciary, entered a bank vault, and met an embalmer.

value system.'

"Every time we've met in a different place. We've been to the United States Senate in Washington, D.C., and the Congress, and the Judiciary. We've had lunch in prison with lifers — it took us a year to get in that place. We've met at a chapel out at Baylor. We've met at a vault in a bank. We watched a veterinarian operating on a dog. We even met at a funeral home."

Paul grins as he recalls the last encounter. "The kids joke with me like you wouldn't believe. Our host at the funeral home was explaining how to embalm somebody. He had a high-pitched voice, and he said, 'I'll tell you, I would be delighted to do you, Mr. Meyer, when it comes your time.' Brother, he freaked me out! I told the kids, 'Man, that guy can't wait to get his hands on me.' Anyhow, I said to him, 'I'll tell you how much I appreciate your offer. It would be my pleasure for you to do me when my time comes.' And you know what? His face lit up!"

If Paul Meyer's presence lives on after his death, however, it won't be thanks to embalming, but to the people he's influenced. Recently he has become involved in plans to attack the problem of teenage pregnancy. In 1988, Paul had established a program called Passport to Success to provide college and technical school scholarships for economically disadvantaged young people in his county. When staff members reported to him that one of the pressing problems in Waco schools was teenage pregnancy, he agreed that something positive should be done.

Passport to Success staff members are working with several other organizations in the county and with the schools to design a program that will influence teenagers to postpone sexual involvement until marriage. A pilot program now in place for one small segment of youth has shown promise, and ways are being sought to expand it. One of the features will be harnessing peer pressure to work for sexual abstinence instead of against it. "Peer pressure is powerful," Paul says. "Why not use it positively instead of negatively?"

Even in organizations he did not set up, Paul takes a direct and creative interest. Pondering his investment in leadership training, he realized in 1984 that he could benefit Haggai Institute most effectively by funding its development department.

"I made the remark to the trustees — I just joked — I said 'Your top man's going to die. He's not going to live forever. And in my personal opinion it's going to take ten people, maybe twenty, to take his place in fund-raising alone. He just happens to be that good. Besides, he's the one who started this. It wouldn't make any difference how great somebody else was at raising money, nobody can do it like he can. No one else has the commitment, the conviction, the focus, or the story. He knows more world leaders, and knows more people — he's so far ahead it's incredible.'"

Paul started a fund to employ a permanent development staff strong enough, eventually, to take the founder's place.

"For one thing," says Paul, "a leader needs to have his head in writing. He needs to put down everything about this ministry on paper. Half of it is in his back pocket, and the rest of it is in his head. If we want to perpetuate the idea he's introduced, he needs to spend his time coaching and training other people, not raising money."

For another thing, Paul knows just how hard it is to win a

donor's loyalty. "Development work takes patience. Look how long it took them to reel me in. You wouldn't call me a fast sell. I'm cautious about where I put my money. I'm generous, but I want to make sure I do it right, maximize the potential."

Paul's not kidding about his caution — it's legendary. In the early days, Haggai Institute put on a testimonial dinner for Paul Meyer. On his return to Waco, he mailed a check for $100 — something far less than we had expected. He treats his donations as carefully as he'd treat venture capital. Once he has done his "due diligence" and concludes the organization meets his criteria, he gives with unspeakable generosity. And with sound results.

2. Control the future

Look at this rough breakdown of Paul Meyer's timetable over his 70-hour productive week:

PLANNING	15%	Strategy, scheduling, deadlines.
EVALUATION	20%	Evaluating, delegating.
REVIEWING	15%	Reports, ideas, trends.
ADMINISTRATION	20%	Hands on management, priorities and major decisions.
PERSONAL	30%	Family, church, playing.

You'll notice two things.

One, he has achieved a level of efficiency that permits him to spend almost a third of his time in nonprofessional activity (with family, church, or private hobbies). And two, half of his directly related work time — that is, half of the time/energy resource he devotes to running his businesses and philanthropy — goes to *future planning*.

Not all planning helps. I've learned from observing Paul Meyer that most people make the mistake of scheduling their future in "blocks." That is, they think of investments as lengths of time that fall between the naming of a goal and its final accomplishment. Then they chop up that time-block into a series of smaller time-blocks, assigning each little block to a different stage in the investment process. So, for instance, obtaining and paying back a loan becomes a lengthy three-part business consisting of looking for a deal, making a contract, and paying back what you owe. In diagram form it looks like this:

```
LOOK FOR      TAKE              PAY LOAN
BEST DEAL     LOAN              BACK

|——————————|————|————————————————————|
```

But in reality we invest our resources not in blocks of time, but in *points* of time. A well-organized search for the best deal can take as little as an hour; signing for the loan takes minutes; paying it back can be done by direct debit — an arrangement that, once set up, makes no demands on your time at all. Add together the total time/ energy you devote to getting and paying off the loan, and you may find it takes no longer than watching a movie.

We need to think of the process, therefore, not as a line divided up into blocks, but as a series of points, single entries in the diary, pinprick investments:

```
LOOK FOR      TAKE       PAY LOAN
BEST DEAL     LOAN       BACK
▼             ▼          ▼
```

The difference matters because if you schedule your time/ energy in blocks everything takes longer. As Parkinson said in his famous law, "work expands to fill the time available for its completion." Allocate eight hours to a three-hour project, and the project will swell obligingly to waste your day.

To plan efficiently, you need to keep a tight rein on your time allocations. The rules are straightforward: do only what is necessary, and do it only at the necessary time.

From there on, you can manage time/energy resources with nothing more sophisticated than a diary. You require only a method of pre-scheduling your investments and reminding yourself when they fall due — plus, of course, the discipline to review your daily agenda and carry forward to tomorrow the tasks you couldn't complete today.

For people on Paul Meyer's level, of course, a diary will no longer do. Paul Meyer uses a blend of methods for keeping track.

"All the financial information is basically on computers. Then I have the three-ring binders — one on every single company. I have all my personal goals written down, broken down into different areas of my life. The business ones, of course, I have delegated, and have different people working on them. The very personal information I keep in my confidential binders. I review these on average once a week. My giving goals I look at maybe twice a month. My prayer goals I look at every single day."

Paul operates a highly developed goals program, involving him in extensive interaction with staff. His assistants regularly condense information on his business and philanthropy and enter them in his system of binders, dividing and labeling each binder for ease of access. Financial statements are printed and replaced monthly.

A talk with Linda Peterson, Paul's personal assistant, is revealing of his organizational habits:

JH: How does Paul handle interoffice memos?

LP: Usually when Paul replies to a memo he simply writes on it and returns it. That saves time.

JH: Then you file it?

LP: I keep a copy of all outgoing memos.

JH: How much time does it take to do the filing?

LP: Well, there are several files that have to be kept up-to-date on a daily basis. Other things—the less urgent ones—I often have to save up and do when he's out of town.

He has two command files for giving. One outlines key data on recipient organizations and includes an assortment of press cuttings and photos. The other gives a series of incredibly detailed breakdowns of amounts both pledged and given in the current year. A summary page lists in percentage order the 21 organizations Paul supports at a level exceeding $10,000 per year, showing for every month the amount committed or actually transferred. Other breakdowns detail the term of each donation, the payment interval, the date and purpose of the pledge, and the source of the contribution. Not infrequently, he will send a spreadsheet with his donation — a kind of unspoken challenge to the recipient to keep straight and meticulous accounts.

Once you actually own a corporation, of course, tracking almost has to become a shared activity. The challenge for Paul has been to keep pushing the minor functions away from himself.

He well remembers a visit in early years from Hong Kong businessman Henry Tseng, a user of the SMI program. Tseng, on a trip to the United States, wanted to extend his thanks to Paul in person.

"You taught me something," he said, "and now I want to teach you something. Just let me observe you."

He observed Paul for several hours, and Paul went about his work as though Tseng weren't there. At one point he gave one of his managers a raft of detailed instructions. When he got through, Henry Tseng said, "I feel sorry for that man."

"Tom? Why?"

"Because he becomes a lesser person every time he talks to you. You tell him what to do and you leave nothing to his imagination, nothing for him to do. He becomes less and less a thinking person, and more and more a robot."

Paul felt bad because he had a lot of respect for Tom.

Henry Tseng went on, "Where are the company books?"

"In the safe," replied Paul.

"Which is. . .?"

"In the closet."

Tseng laughed out loud. "I thought so. You don't trust anybody else with the books, eh?"

He went on to prove that Paul had been over-controlling, and hadn't delegated anything of significance to anyone. Almost as soon as Tseng had gone, Paul called in Tom and had him take away all the materials on sales promotion and sales training. Henceforward these became Tom's responsibility. Paul went through almost the entire operation delegating this way. Until then he'd done virtually everything; he'd been a one-man band. "After Henry Tseng came," he says, "I set out to organize, deputize, and supervise."

As a result, Paul can clear in ninety minutes a desk-load of work that would take the average executive half a day. "See these tabs?" he says, flicking the edge of a binder. "This stuff is for me to read — project reports submitted by the people directly answerable to me. There're fifteen of them. Key people who interface with me, like Joe Baxter. This is a project report from him." Paul — working as he talks — makes his response to Baxter's memo. It's pithy and fills just four lines. Often he fires off a string of memos, sometimes only a sentence long, requesting a call, or asking for a specific piece of information.

At his companies' master switchboard they keep a master book of everyone Paul Meyer has ever called. It's hooked up to his phone from seven in the morning until midnight. Linda Peterson makes a record of each call and files it, so two years from now he'll know exactly whom he called, when he made the call, and what was said.

Delegation has now become spontaneous and routine. If a distributor writes to Paul outlining some problems with the distributorship, Linda Peterson handles it with the president of the respective company with which the distributor works. She sends a memo requesting that the president and the marketing director get together, research it, discuss it, and then give Paul a synopsis of the problem and their proposed solution. All Paul has to do is agree with their plan or suggest something different.

Behind this, of course, lies the principle that a decision-maker's function majors on making decisions, not fumbling around looking for background information. By the time a company problem requires Paul Meyer's input, all the facts are in place, all the alternatives have been researched, every detail he needs lies at his fingertips. It boosts his already high productivity at an exponential rate.

"He's very detail-minded," says Peterson. "He works very hard. After all the years I've had the privilege of working with him, I'm amazed how much the man is capable of doing in a day. He just has so many things going all the time, and he works feverishly at every project."

3. Never stop at mistakes

You may not know that ostriches are fast becoming big business in America.

Ostriches provide not only feathers but also shoe leather and meat. The American government buys ostrich feathers in quantity to clean sensitive computer parts; General Motors buys them to give car bodies a final dusting before the paint goes on. Ostrich meat has twice the protein content of beef, and less fat and cholesterol than chicken.

Paul at his ostrich farm with the author, Leslie Meyer and Steve Justice. Everything the ostrich farm earns is given to charity.

Yet in 1989, America had an estimated ostrich population of only 4,000, of which only 500 were productive adult breeders, compared to an estimated 100,000 in South Africa. In an expanding industry, therefore, a solid market already existed for breeding birds. Paul Meyer knew an opportunity when he saw one and developed a farm on the Chisholm Trail.

Initially it looked like a complete flop.

"Everybody thought I'd slipped a cog and now I needed a keeper. Because I bought a pair of birds for $40,000, and one of them died in two weeks. Then I got 48 chicks, and I was supposed to make $3,000 apiece for them, and 40 chicks died in two weeks. Finally I said, 'It serves me right. I didn't do my homework.'"

He went to visit the farms, sent his personnel to all the seminars, read everything he could find on ostrich farming, contacted all the top veterinarians. His overall goals remained sound; the problems lay in the technical intermediary goals involved in successful stock raising. For Paul, therefore, the loss of a batch of chicks wasn't a failure: it was an education. And the education continues.

"Last year I made $800,000 in that business. And I made

$100,000 last month. So this year I expect to make a million. But even though we're a leader in the industry, and I'm building a business and it's profitable, I admit that we're amateurs. We're beginners. We're just learning. I just think that's part of the process."

Paul Meyer has a favorite saying: "You win some, you lose some, and some get rained out." Life is like a game. What matters isn't the individual play or even the match, but winning over the long-haul. You can't eliminate all setbacks. Yet as Paul says, "The temporary setback is there so you'll learn something. I just assume that's part of every deal you get into."

The trick is being ready to adjust, reevaluate, shift emphasis, fine-tune, reorganize. In that way, dream planning resembles sailing. If you don't constantly take new bearings, the uncontrollable factors — the winds and currents — will force you off course. The art of good seamanship doesn't lie in setting your course so perfectly that you avoid the currents. That's impossible. It lies in predicting, measuring, and countering their effects.

The principle applies to all dream planning. If one road turns into a cul-de-sac, then reroute. Try another road. If you run into blockages everywhere, reassess your program, shift the parameters, see if there are other objectives capable of meeting your long-term requirements. If the front door won't open, try the back; if the back door sticks, break a window.

"Ninety percent of all those who fail in life," says Paul, "are not actually defeated; they have simply quit."

A touching and true story of my father's friend, H. Framer Smith, illustrates the point.

About the time the First World War broke out, he arrived at Moody Bible Institute in Chicago with one wife, one baby, one battered jalopy — and one eye. He had virtually no money, so he supported his family while he studied by doing night jobs, snatching sleep when he could. Once he operated an apartment-house elevator. He would read until his eye could take no more, and then sleep until somebody rang the bell.

One afternoon the Moody Bible Institute employment department, Framer Smith's employment agency, summoned him. The director said, "Lady So-and-So from England has been living in one of our guest apartments for several months. She's getting on in years, and demands additional service to that which we provide. Four young men have worked for her and left because, they said nothing pleases her. But she does pay well."

Being heartily sick of sitting in elevators, Framer Smith took the job. He found his predecessors more or less correct in their assessment. Nothing satisfied this lady. She made him rescrub the bathtub. She made him straighten the fringes at the edge of the rug a second time. She made him remove and replace the dishes and flatware in a special pattern in the drawers. At times he felt frustration bordering on rage. But, as his agency director had promised, the job paid well, and he had a strong work ethic, so he kept on.

After a few months she asked to see him.

She said, "Young man, you need to hear what I have to say, and I hope you'll never forget it."

He thought, "Uh-oh, here it comes."

She continued, "I have put you through the crucible. The others gave up, failed. No matter how mercilessly I pressured you, you took it. You won. I trust you completely. In a few days I shall return to my native England. I won't be needing your services any longer."

This was a blow, and Framer Smith's face showed it.

But the lady went on, "Don't worry, you'll have all the funds you need. Here's a checkbook for an account I've set up in your name. I shall maintain a sufficient balance to handle all your needs at all times until you finish your education."

Framer Smith earned undergraduate and graduate degrees, becoming both a Doctor of Philosophy and a Doctor of Sacred Theology. His patience and determination won out.

Those same qualities seem to be part of the Meyer family heritage. Paul Meyer's eldest son, Jim, now a lawyer, recalls vividly how his father taught him self-motivation. No painstaking assembly of bicycle parts, but a chart on the bedroom wall challenging the child to replace "I can't" with "I can" and "I don't think" with "I know."

"Whatever we tried to do," says Jim Meyer, "we were to do our best. The point was not winning or losing; the point was trying your hardest. Don't be a quitter. Finish what you start. All that stuff I carried through. I remember training to get a pilot's license. I figured out when I was halfway through that I didn't really want to be a pilot, but I got the license anyway because I didn't want to quit.

The same thing when I got my karate black belt. I just forced myself to keep going." He chuckles. "That's probably what got me through law school."

And the training trickles down. By the time Jim's son Mike was a sophomore in high school he knew he wanted to be a baseball player. He deliberately transferred from a 400-strong private school to a 3,700-strong public school because the colleges would be more likely to see him in a larger school. And he's quick to notice lethargy in others. Not long ago, Jim took him out for baseball practice with a school friend.

"I started throwing the baseball to Mike's friend, who is also a college baseball player, and this kid said, 'I just can't hit it, I just can't do this.' And Mike kind of glanced up at me, as if to say, 'Oh, gosh, did you just hear what Chad said?'"

The proud father chuckles. "You see in the Meyer family 'can't' is a curse word."[15]

And so it should be. Why? Because goal-setters see the craft of goal-setting and the language of "can't" as mutually exclusive. Especially *giving* goal-setters like Paul J. Meyer.

7

THE PEOPLE-CENTERED GIVER

S ays Paul Meyer, "I've seen my whole life as one of helping people. When I sold insurance I was helping people. When I was working with Word, I was helping people. I got into the self-improvement business to help people use more of their God-given potential."

It's no accident that he talks of philanthropy in explicitly personal terms.   The word "philanthropy" can mislead.   It portrays philanthropists as a kind of subcategory of the human race, equipped with especially deep pockets and especially generous hands, for the purpose of sprinkling cash among the poor and needy. Clearly this is nonsense. It represents philanthropy as a kind of clay sculpting: as though it meant making things out of money — hospitals, consignments of grain, cures for cancer, and so on. But philanthropy means far more than financing a bricks-and-mortar project and then having your name chiseled into the lintel. *What* you give matters far, far less than the *people* you give it to.

Andrew Carnegie, one of America's most famous givers, practiced a fundamental people-orientation. Hence his support of public utilities: parks, concert halls, organs, baths, and church buildings. To those with enough money he recommended the establishment or endowment of universities, technical institutes, museums, libraries, observatories, hospitals, medical schools, and laboratories, "and other institutions connected with the alleviation of human suffering, and especially with the prevention rather than the cure of human ills."[16]

The writer Earl V. Pierce develops this same point when he talks about money as "stored-up man." Exchanging time/energy for money, Pierce would argue, involves a storing of our essential nature because the true value of money can only be realized by exchanging it for something personal.

He illustrates this by recalling a visit to a friend's house. "I love to see my children eat," the friend confided over dinner. "He might have said," comments Pierce, "that he loved to hear them eat, for they were going at it vigorously." Nevertheless, Pierce noted with approval that this man was investing his monetary resources in (exchanged into, we could say) the relational resources that were his children. Money might belong to a "lower world," but "it was a great satisfaction to see all of this investment in the lower world would be going back again into the higher world of personality."

To Pierce, the true value of your wealth emerges in the use you put it to. He's right. Sheer logic compels one to consider a life devoted to money-making for its own sake as a life lost:

> Money gambled, drunk, smoked, frittered away into that which has no ultimate good in it, is so much of life utterly lost. Money can be spent for oneself or others, on vacations, recreation, education and culture, in ways that literally become re-creation. "Unless a man is as mindful of the output of his business in public benefit as of its intake in private benefit, he is on no higher moral level than the grazing ox," says one. But we can at least profit by the death of the ox, but not from the death of a selfish man.[17]

In the lobby of the Shangri-la Hotel in Singapore a few years ago, I ran into an old friend and a financial wizard, Max Rondoni. I asked Max a question I often ask people with business acumen: "What is your definition of wealth?"

Max responded, "Wealth is the sum of what you have spent on yourself and what you have given away after you have provided prudently — though not lavishly — for your children. In many instances, people have not spent enough on themselves. In more instances, they have not given away enough. Actually, true wealth *utilizes* money. If you have 40 suits and you wear only six of them, you are paying storage on 34 suits which, in fact, you have no more benefit from than if you had never purchased them."

You may or may not agree with Pierce and Rondoni on where to draw the lines: the bon vivant who enjoys a bottle of Möet et Chandon before dinner and a fat Havana after it will hardly look on these luxuries as "so much of life utterly lost." And yet the moral marker will not be entirely dislodged. We all have to prioritize our use of resources, and, in choosing which investments to make, the potential of some investments to be "re-creative" will always tend to promote them over others.

All of us can list what we consider wise and foolish uses for money. We all agree that some resource exchanges give us a better deal. And one of the main reasons why giving matters so much derives from the resource we call "relationships," which is surely among the most valuable. Does not this resource swell powerfully when we give? Does not giving (in every sense, not just the financial) turn money and time/energy into relationships? Does it not underpin and fuel reciprocity? Does not doing something for another without seeking any return lay the ground and basis of friendship? Why else is generosity so highly praised?

In 1993, Walter Annenberg, ex-ambassador and billionaire, made the largest one-time gift to private education that America has ever seen: $365 million: $25 million went to Harvard, $100 million to his alma mater, the Peddie Preparatory School, and $120 million apiece to the communications programs at the Universities of Southern California and Pennsylvania. His reason? "I'm interested in the young people because the character of our country will be shaped by young people in the days ahead."

At 85 years of age, Annenberg knew the absolute importance of investing money in *people*. Today's students become tomorrow's decision-makers. Society has a direct and compelling interest in teaching them well.

Every branch of philanthropy circles back to people. Though the park bench bears a plaque commemorating the donor, it functions as more than a mere memorial: it perpetuates a place for comfort and rest. True, you can find plenty of charities devoted to the salvation of the panda, the preserving of a marsh habitat for some rare seabird, or the prevention of medical experimentation on live monkeys. But even here, you have difficulty in isolating the interests of the animals from the interests of the *people* whose lives are enriched by their survival and welfare. The extinction of the panda would occasion a real loss to every person on the planet.

So giving is essentially relational — feeding and inextricably bound into personal relationships. When we give, we need to think "who," not "what." And because of that, certain useful ground rules define good giving.

1. Don't give beggars dimes

"It is often easier," writes Earl Pierce, "to give a beggar a dime than it is to follow him up and see what it is he really needs."

Andrew Carnegie expressed much the same opinion:

> It were better for mankind that the millions of the rich was thrown into the sea than so spent as to encourage the slothful, the drunken, the unworthy. Of every thousand dollars spent in so called charity today, it is probable that $950 is unwisely spent; so spent, indeed, as to produce the very evils which it proposes to mitigate or cure. A well known writer of philosophic books admitted the other day that he had given a quarter of a dollar to a man who approached him as he was coming to visit the house of his friend. He knew nothing of the habits of this beggar; knew not the use that would be made of this money, although he had every reason to suspect that it would be spent improperly.

This man, Carnegie goes on to suggest, "only gratified his own feelings, saved himself from annoyance — and this was probably one of the most selfish and very worst actions of his life."

All in all, Carnegie came down rather hard on the charity of his day. But he wasn't alone. In the original version of *Wealth*, which Carnegie sent to *The North American Review* in May of 1889, he had estimated that $900 of every thousand was wasted. Yet the *Review* editor, Allen Thorndyke Rice, recommended he revise the figure upward to $950 — the only change Rice required in the whole manuscript.

Of course you can see how the psychology of a begging encounter works. Giving a dime — or a dollar, even ten dollars — is easier than addressing the real problem, because it requires a smaller investment of your resources. Money seems less valuable than time: basically you give the beggar some cash so he'll quit hassling you. Nevertheless, as you replace your pocketbook you know you've betrayed yourself, that you're walking away with the word "sucker" written all over your face. Like Carnegie, you're not convinced the money will go to buy the beggar a meal. But even if he's a bona fide destitute and doesn't take your cash to the nearest liquor store, you've only bought him another few hours of nourishment. To give him "what he needs" — a job, perhaps, education, shelter, long-term personal support — seems quite beyond your power. Such need opens like a chasm at your feet. To toss a few coins into it seems futile, even insulting.

This is not the moment, however, to throw up your hands in despair. You *can* distinguish a beggar's real needs from the particular request he makes of you on the street. If you put a high priority in your giving list on the needs of the poor and homeless, you can find effective ways to satisfy them. And the same with any other group whose circumstances make them a target for financial giving.

Long before Paul Meyer and his Passport to Success staff began to plan a program to prevent teenage pregnancy, he had attacked the problem from the other end by contributing to the building and renovation costs of a home for unmarried mothers.

Angel House, named after a girl who needed a place to stay during her crisis pregnancy, stands on Waco's 33rd Street near the Hillcrest Baptist Medical Center. It can house up to six residents. Though licensed by the state, this nonprofit organization receives only private funding from churches, individuals, businesses, service clubs, and foundations. An independent board of governors oversee it.

It provides its residents, aged between 13 and 24, with encouragement and schooling. It accepts women at any stage of pregnancy. They participate in running the home — making menus, preparing food, and keeping house. Of five babies born at the home in 1991, only two were put up for adoption. Angel House remains the only home of its kind in central Texas, and there is a waiting list to get in.

Practice strategic giving. Paul considers it cruel to make one donation to a struggling enterprise if you have no intention of following up with another. However emphatically you stress that it is a one-time gift, the agency will expect and hope and dream that other gifts will follow. One of the major headaches for those who give their lives to helping others develops from the uncertainty over future funding: the next financial year is an overgrown jungle path, and hacking your way through it with fund-raising uses up vast resources of time and effort that could have been directed to the work itself.

Timing also plays a crucial part in maximizing the benefits of the gift. Too many donors feel that their generosity relieves them of any responsibility to give at times convenient to the beneficiary. In particular, in America many donors making larger gifts will wait until the end of the year to check their tax situation before fulfilling a pledge. Again, though, as in so many respects, Paul Meyer is exceptional. He confirms his commitments at the beginning of the year, then gives the money in regular monthly installments. This enables his beneficiaries to plan securely and avoid borrowing to cover the deficit build up. Enormous savings result not only in the beneficiary's time/energy investment, but also in the percentages that would otherwise slip away in interest payments.

2. Do only what's needed

In 1988, when he established the Passport to Success Foundation, a five-million-dollar educational trust to provide post-secondary education for economically disadvantaged youth, Paul Meyer was thinking mainly about teenagers — recent high school graduates. The program stipulated that scholarship recipients be members of the Waco Boys and Girls Club. He reasoned that this requirement would make it possible for program staff members to keep tabs on future scholarship recipients, to encourage them to stay in school and make the best grades they could make. Also, the Club had long been a favorite project of his.

The program was announced near the end of May, and the first students to begin college in the fall were quickly identified. During the summer, a young man who was employed as program director at one of the branches of the Waco Boys and Girls Club contacted Paul to ask if he might also be considered for a scholarship. David Hurtado had been a member of the Club as a child. After finishing high school, he had taken a job at the Club and had attended college part-time. He had completed two years at McLennan Community College. But while going to school, he had married and started a family. He knew he needed to go on to the university, but his salary just would not stretch that far. He had become discouraged and had decided that he would probably never be able to complete a degree and could never expect to hold a higher position.

Paul asked Gladys Hudson, president of Passport to Success, to look into his qualifications. The executive director of the Club gave

Paul with the first Passport to Success group, in September 1980, and meeting President Ronald Reagan in 1988. PTS helps Waco's economically disadvantaged young people get a college education, and has sent young people to places as different as the American Truck Driving School and the Vogue College of Cosmetology.

David an excellent recommendation, and Paul authorized a scholarship to pay Hurtado's tuition and fees to attend Baylor University. David immediately enrolled and stuck with both his studies and his job until he earned his degree.

While he was still working on his degree, David was promoted to branch director. A year or two after his degree was conferred, David Hurtado was made executive director of the three branches of the Waco Boys and Girls Club. "Thanks to Paul Meyer and Passport to Success," Hurtado says, "I regained my belief in my ability to succeed. I was able to get the education I needed; so I was ready for promotion when an opening came." David Hurtado is one of the most enthusiastic supporters of Passport to Success. He encourages all the young people at the Club to join PTS and begin planning for a brighter future.

This kind of motivating, catalytic approach to philanthropy typifies Paul Meyer. He also employs it in far more informal ways. Recently he heard about a man who had fallen on hard times.

"I'd never met the man," Paul says. "But I gave him $850 a month, got him a car, gave him a place to live. I'm going to take care of him for six months. This man is 49. He doesn't even know how to get help from a church or from the Salvation Army. We've got to teach him how to get some help. But better than that, I will help him preserve his dignity by helping him get a job."

Later, L.D. Tanner, an associate of Paul's, said to the man, "Paul might help you a little bit more. What would you like to do?"

He replied, "I'm a writer. My dream is that I could make a living with a mom-and-pop operation, with a weekly newspaper in a small town in Texas."

Paul's response?

"We'll help him buy a small paper in a small town. We'll help him get the money. And I've still never met him. I don't know who he is. But," he adds with a smile, "I'm not a fool. I had him checked out. L.D. Tanner is the best of the best in getting information on people. I don't give my money to people who wave a little sign 'Will work for food.' And I've never sent a dime to a TV evangelist or for some appeal sent by mass direct mail."

3. Keep relationships sweet

David Hurtado furnishes only one of the success stories of Passport to Success. Are they all like that?

Paul Meyer becomes pensive. "That's a good question," he replies. "If you asked me, 'Is there anything you've ever done that has completely shocked you?' I'd have to say it's my experience of giving to the very poor. Sometimes parents will say, 'Hey, we're poor. That's good enough for us. We're getting along just fine. We don't need anyone over here meddling.' Sometimes I argue. I tell the children, 'Let me explain something to you. The way things are now, you're going to make minimum wage the rest of your life. Okay? For fifty years. That's all you are going to get if you don't get an education. If you'll go two years to school — you don't have to go four years, you don't have to go seven years, just for two years — you can be a nurse or whatever else and earn all the way up to twelve dollars an hour. You can make three times as much by studying for just two years. That's a good deal. And then if you want to go above that, you can. There's no limit.' And you know what? Sometimes they just don't see it. They turn it down. The program is six years old now, and I've got only 125 young people in college."

This problem has a range of causes. Many of the young people eligible for the program had never considered the possibility of college. As a result, they had felt little compulsion to do well in high school. There was a large drop-out rate in the city's schools. Some parents seemed reluctant to believe the program would benefit their children. Many of the young people had no family role models who had attended college. They could not visualize themselves as college students.

But although the fourteen young people receiving degrees in 1994 and 1995 have until now been the program's largest single intake, the signs indicate that persistence is beginning to pay off. The freshman class in 1994 numbers 9; but the high school seniors already preparing for college entrance in 1995 include 28 students, and the high school juniors now enrolled number 80. "I tell you," says Paul, who is, after all, one of the country's premier salesmen, "this has been a hard sell, but we are beginning to see real results."

This story shows how hard Paul Meyer works to give "on the level." He unfailingly ranks others as equal to himself, whatever their social background or financial circumstances. His top executives, his yardman, and his cleaning staff all receive the same generous, considerate, and courteous treatment. He never makes the mistake of spoiling his giving with condescension.

I can confirm from my own childhood how vital such sensitivity is. One morning in the winter of 1931, I remember coming down to breakfast — and finding no breakfast on the table. My not quite seven-year-old mind whirred. "What's wrong?" I thought. Outside in Kalamazoo, Michigan, the worst snow blizzard in recorded history had paralyzed the city. No cars could move. The snow had drifted up to the second story roof-edge of our house. Not only could I see no breakfast, I felt cold.

Always inquisitive, I asked Dad what was happening. I learned he had put the last piece of coke on the fire. Our fuel and food supplies were both exhausted. There remained only eight ounces of milk for my baby brother Tom and some condiments which one could not use without a regular meal.

"Daddy, what are we going to eat?" I wanted to know.

"We'll have our devotions first, John Edmund," he said in such a way as to let me know I should not ask questions.

He then read Scripture, our daily family practice. After the Bible reading, we knelt for prayer. Dad prayed earnestly for the family, the relatives, friends — especially those with special needs, the "missionaries of the cross," those suffering the blizzard without adequate shelter. Then he prayed something like this: "Lord, Thou knowest we've just put the last piece of coke on the fire. There's nothing more to burn in the fireplace. If it can please Thee, provide fuel. If not, Thy will be done. We thank Thee for warm clothes and bed covers which will keep us comfortable even without the fire. And, Thou knowest we have no food except milk for Baby Thomas. If it can please Thee. . ."

For the last several minutes my father's voice had been almost drowned by a commotion outside. Now we heard a pounding on the front door. Someone was shouting at us, but the snow packed in front of the door muffled the sound. Finally the man outside brushed away enough snow that he could peer through the frosty window pane. Ice had sealed the door, he said. Dad jumped up. The man outside pushed; Dad pulled; and soon they opened the door — bringing an avalanche into the entrance hall.

My dad, who didn't remember ever having seen the man, said, "May I help you?"

"No, no, Reverend, I awakened at four o'clock with you on my mind. I couldn't get the truck out of the garage, so I harnessed the horses to the sleigh to bring you some food and wood."

This dear man — a farmer with gnarled hands — brought in a feast of milk, eggs, butter, pork chops, grain, homemade bread, and a host of other items which now, more than 63 years later, have escaped my memory. Oh yes — and he brought nearly a cord of wood.

He told my father, "I heard you preach in Allegan three years ago, and the Lord has brought you to my mind many times since then. I hope you're not offended by this intrusion."

Dad insisted he stay to get warm and enjoy breakfast with us. Obviously, the fact I'm writing this lets you know what an indelible impression this event made upon me. I can't put into words the joy in my boyish heart as Dad thanked the Lord for our friend, the food, and the wood.

Let me add parenthetically that Dad and Mother had reared us with strict instructions never to discuss family financial needs. They would keep reminding us, "God is the Provider." Consequently our benefactor had no way of knowing about our critical need for food and heat. As years passed on, I reflected on the words of the Psalmist:

> *I have never seen the righteous forsaken nor God's seed begging bread (Psalm 37:25).*

Throughout all the years of the depression, Mother and Dad never failed to give at least a tenth of their meager income. Lack of financial resources never damaged their self-esteem, nor bred in them a trace of anger or resentment. Nevertheless, note the self-effacing humility of the farmer who brought us our breakfast. It never occurred to him to look down on us. We were his neighbors, his friends, his equals. He gave "across," not "down."

I stress the point because giving can so easily mask a selfish pride. "The word charity carries opprobrium," comments Earl Pierce. "No one likes to use it, except the dispensers of it."[18] The feel-good factor in giving can be so strong that a donor ceases to consider the psychological cost to the beneficiary. You can end up savoring too much the role of Lord or Lady Bountiful, and forget that the person you give to is a person just like yourself, with the same sense of dignity and entitled to the same respect. All the more vital, then, to internalize the courtesy which that old farmer knew by instinct and which Paul Meyer has honed to perfection: a determination not to underline differences of financial status by standing on some lofty psychological pedestal when you give.

One more key area of concern for the giver — and one that

many givers worry about — involves the family, and particularly the children. One person's charitable gift, after all, can look like another person's disinheritance. Paul Meyer remains acutely aware of the dangers here.

"I have friends who are wealthy, and their wealth has created family problems. For instance, the sons resent the father's generosity. They think he's giving away their money. So I'm taking time to explain to my children the importance of giving. I'm expecting to set up everything so that, whatever they do, they perpetuate that. If my sons don't have the same heart and spirit, if I fail to pass that on, then I've really done something wrong."

Paul Meyer's sons — and daughters — are picking up the giving habit. Talk, for instance, to Janna, or to Billy, and they'll both tell you that what really impresses them about their dad is his Christian faith and his generosity. Billy, who owns extensive real estate, says he's learned from Paul both to give and to teach others to give. He has his father's faith. And the same commitment to his own children. He even gave up his beloved car racing so he could spend more time with them.

Andrew Carnegie pondered the same challenge of passing values on to the next generation, and proposed a typically pragmatic solution.

Provided that the next generation shows sufficient public spirit, Carnegie argues, "the duty of the parent is to see that such are provided for *in moderation*." The italics are his. Of the wisdom of passing down huge sums to one's children he was decidedly dubious. He goes on: "There are instances of millionaires' sons unspoiled by wealth, who, being rich, still perform great services in the community. Such are the very salt of the earth, as valuable as, unfortunately, they are rare; still it is not the exception, but the rule that men must regard, and, looking at the usual result of enormous sums conferred upon legatees, the thoughtful man must shortly say, 'I would as soon leave to my son a curse as the almighty dollar,' and admit to himself that it is not the welfare of the children, but family pride, which inspires these enormous legacies.'"

4. Impact the world for good

Giving became a truly global concern for the first time in 1910

Impacting the world for good. John Edmund Haggai presents Jane and Paul with the World Changers Award at Haggai Institute's 200th session, Maui, 1994.

— thanks mostly to the work of a remarkable man: Dr. John R. Mott.

As chief executive officer of the YMCA, Mott had seen an unprecedented opportunity for expansion in Asia. Across the world new nations were forming, and the YMCA, being international, interdenominational, and already indigenous in most countries, possessed a unique platform on which people of all religions and no religion could come under the impress of Christian thinking and values.

Mott initially calculated that to set up the necessary 49 YMCA centers would cost $1,080,000, and promptly submitted his plan to John D. Rockefeller with a request for $540,000. To evaluate the project, Rockefeller dispatched an assistant, Dr. Burton (later president of the University of Chicago), on a world tour that lasted the better part of a year, and then gave Mott the sum he'd asked for. Meanwhile, in the hot summer of 1910, Mott went to Beverly, Massachusetts, to ask if President William Howard Taft would be willing to address a conference on the "Worldwide Expansion of the YMCA." Taft not only agreed; he asked Mott to convene the conference at the White House.

"This," the Commissioner of the District of Columbia said in his opening remarks to the conference on October 20, "is an absolutely unique gathering. . . . All former gatherings which have been held here were really limited to the United States. This morning we assemble in the interest of the whole world and are looking out from this high place upon all the nations of the earth."

After a great many men had said their piece — including the President and the Army Chief of Staff — Mott rose to outline his financial challenge. "There are two ways of going about his matter," he announced. "One. . .is to let forty-nine separate appeals loose upon the good people of the United States and Canada. The other plan is to consolidate all of these appeals, and to come to the friends of this world once for this period of three years." The YMCA, he said, supported the latter option, and "announce today their conviction that the sum of $1,515,000 should be secured for the providing of these forty-nine buildings, for some ten nations which we are seeking to help, such as China, Japan, Korea, India, the Philippines, certain parts of Latin America, Russia, and the Turkish Empire. . . ."

The estimated costs had risen. But the response was immediate, and some months later when the fund was closed Mott had amassed over $2,000,000 — half a million more than he'd asked for. As Europe emerged from the Great War and the pace of life quickened in Asia, a further appeal realized over $6,000,000.

That these colossal amounts were raised so fast remains a testimony to Mott's skill as a fund-raiser and motivator. But it also reflects an enduring fact about philanthropy: that giving and the achievements it generates are quite simply exciting. Mott's gift of communicating this excitement in all its depth and richness motivated these people of great capacity to release the necessary funds.

His first encounter with Andrew Carnegie illustrates the effect well. On a visit to New York to see Cleveland H. Dodge, Mott mentioned in passing that he and Carnegie had never met.

"I will take you to see Andy now," Dodge replied immediately.

When they arrived at the steel magnate's residence on Riverside Drive, Carnegie was out. He turned up some time later in golf clothes and a foul mood, having just lost a game.

"Lord, what a day!" he said, landing on the sofa with a thud.

"I have brought you a man whom you ought to know," Dodge said, and introduced Mott.

"What has he got to say?" demanded Carnegie.

Mott immediately told him about the vast student migrations, the influence these educated young men would have on the world, and the urgent need to accommodate them.

"You have got a charmer here," smiled Carnegie to Dodge, then added to Mott, "Why are you giving your life to such a work? You are wasting your time. What is your plan?"

Mott briefly outlined his idea of locating key personnel at the great university centers from Tokyo to New York where large numbers of foreign young people were studying. By doing this, he said, he could provide means for them to be exposed to the best instead of the worst side of civilization, and could afford them friendship and stimulating ideals. "And I hope," he concluded, looking at Carnegie, "that you will make a gift of $10,000 a year, for at least two or three years, to make such a plan possible."

"I'll do it if Dodge does," said Carnegie promptly.

Dodge agreed. On the way back Dodge and Mott met another of Dodge's contacts, George Perkins, and told him what had happened.

"That's talking some," responded Perkins. "If you have gotten Carnegie to come across there must be something in the proposition. You ought to let me in on it. I will give you another ten thousand."

The following night, Mott related these events in casual conversation to William Sloane, at a committee meeting in the Union League Club. Sloane added a further eight thousand. In two days, Mott had secured virtually the entire amount required to launch the project, and he'd done it through the sheer contagious excitement of impacting the world for good.

Giving is fun. Not because the giver gains in status by being known as a generous person, but because giving to meet a valid need creates deep satisfaction and fulfillment.

Waco has recently seen the opening of a sanctuary home for abused families. A staggering 26 percent of Texas women of 18 or older — that's 1.3 million — are physically or sexually abused by their spouse or live-in partner. "We've needed this facility for a long time," says Family Abuse Center executive director Lynda Baker, "but we've never had the resources to set something like this up."

The original resources came, via the foundation Christian Missions Concerns, from Paul Piper. Paul Piper told Paul Meyer about the need. Paul Meyer knew that abused women and children needed at least six months of security and safety. He knew also how seldom they got it, and how often lack of funds forced them to return to the situation of abuse. In response, he donated an apartment complex in a secret location, big enough to offer ten units of safe, affordable housing. The home gives the women time to comb the job market and to develop job skills, connecting them with resources like job training and medical help. Rent depends on the individual's income and the number of her dependents.

Paul continues to support the home. Like his friend and associate L.D. Tanner, he desires no public recognition. His satisfaction comes from knowing that his resources tackle the problem at the point of need. In yet one more way he continues to impact the world for good — and without leaving his hometown.

8

THE BUSINESS GIVER

P aul Meyer's experience with National Union Insurance, detailed in Chapter One, ultimately changed the course of his life. He lost everything, but in another sense, he gained everything.

Having just lectured the young Paul on the value of integrity, Claude Pepper rounded off with a quote from Shakespeare's *Othello*:

> Who steals my purse steals trash. . .
> But he that filches from me my good name
> Robs me of that which not enriches him
> and makes me poor indeed.

A few moments later, Hal Roberts pulled up in his Cadillac convertible. Roberts, a pilot by profession and a good friend, had promised to pick up Paul at the courthouse. They drove back to Paul's home in silence. When Roberts pulled up in Paul's street, neither man made a move to get out.

"I've got to sell the house, Hal," said Paul. "I can't make the next payment on it." He paused. "Frankly it's a good thing anyway, because all I ever got out of the insurance business was money."

Roberts nodded. He pulled the gold ring off his fourth finger and handed it to Paul. Inside it were inscribed the words: *This too shall pass.*

Paul handed the ring back and briefly grasped Roberts' arm. "Thanks, Hal."

An hour later the doorbell rang. On the step was Paul's neighbor, Glen McNew.

"Want to take a trip to South Miami Drugstore?"

McNew had never issued such an invitation before. The ever time-conscious Paul, having no other pressing business at hand, said, "Sure."

They sat at the soda fountain and drank a Coke.

"I saw your Cadillacs go," said McNew.

"Yeah?"

"You don't have anything left, do you?"

Paul cocked his head.   "I have three mortgages, and about $90,000 of debt."

Under the counter he felt a wad of notes being pressed into his hand.   "Here, this ought to get you started," said McNew.   He'd given Paul twenty-five one hundred dollar bills.   Neither man spoke.   They were trying to hold back their tears.

Let me pause here to point out that Paul Meyer didn't feel sorry for himself.   He didn't presume upon family or friends to bail him out of his crisis.   He didn't try to camouflage his difficulty with bravado and bluster.   He didn't withdraw from family or friends and seek sanctuary in the make-believe of movies or the superficiality of television soap opera or talk shows. Nor did he do nothing, fabricating fantasies and reaching hopelessly for a false hope that the problem would go away.   He burst into well-considered action.

McNew's gift proved to be pivotal and momentous.   Paul bought himself a $600 second-hand car, and then took a flight to Dallas to meet with Theo Beasley of the Republic National Life Insurance Company.

"You told me to come to you if I ever needed help," Paul said. "Well, now I need it.   I want to borrow fifty thousand dollars."

Beasley didn't miss a beat. "You have it."

"Don't you want to know what I'm going to do with it?"

"No."   Beasley wrote the check.   When Paul asked what sort of note he should sign, Beasley only shrugged his shoulders.   "None," he said.

In fact, Paul wasn't exactly sure what he wanted to do with the loan.   He soon received a number of lucrative offers from other insurance companies — proof, if nothing else, that he had retained his good name.   At first he ruled out a return to the insurance business.   As time went by, though, he changed his mind, and laid plans for a new venture, the Eastern States Life Insurance Company. He and his close friend Bill Armor raised half a million dollars, chose a board of directors and applied for a Florida charter.

To his surprise and annoyance, he received in return an invitation to a Daytona Beach hotel room, and the offer of a charter in exchange for a $25,000 under-the-table payoff.   Paul turned it down flat.   "If I have to start a company by cheating, God knows where I'll end," he said. "You have just closed a chapter in my life." He pulled out of the proposed deal, and returned the money to the investors.

Perhaps Paul Meyer's closest advisor and confidant during this period was his pastor, Dr. Bill Hinson. After the fiasco at Daytona Beach, he told Hinson what he'd said some months earlier to Hal Roberts.

"Insurance got me plenty of money. But you know, Bill, looking back now I realize the money never really interested me. What I liked most about the business was the opportunity to interact with salespeople and clients, talking about motivation, and setting and achieving goals. Sometimes I'd spend thirty minutes selling somebody a life insurance policy, and another two hours showing him how to organize his life."

"If that makes you happy," observed Hinson, "why don't you start a company with that as its purpose?"

"I'd thought of it."

"So why not do it?"

"There's one big obstacle. I have no education in, or information about, the communications industry."

"Then I know someone you should meet," replied Hinson.

That man was Jarrell McCracken, who ten years before had set up Word, Inc., a religious publishing and recording company domiciled in Waco, Texas. When McCracken came to Miami he showed Paul Word's new record library set: the four Gospels, Happy Times, and a Treasure of Sacred Music — 35 records boxed in three or four packages. They sold for $169, of which the salesperson kept $100. "It's commission only," said McCracken. "We can't pay you."

But a salesman of Paul Meyer's caliber didn't need a salary. He agreed to every one of McCracken's terms except the request that he move to Waco. "If I can sell these things in Sodom and Gomorrah," he said (he meant Miami Beach), "I can sell them anywhere."

Over the next ten months he perfected his sales presentation and recruited a Miami sales team. He sold 400 record sets, using the same direct referral system he'd used to sell insurance. Forty thousand dollars didn't touch even ten percent of his previous income. Nevertheless, he now had his franchise system in place. After selling the last of the 400 sets he phoned McCracken to tell him he was ready to move to Waco.

He stayed just two years with Word, becoming National Sales Director for the Library Program.   In a congratulatory letter McCracken acknowledged that Paul had "played a substantial role in our spectacular growth."   Spectacular it certainly was: sales soared by more than 1,000 percent during Paul's association with the company.   In return, Paul received what he'd been looking for — a vital education in the communications business.   When the two years were up, he left Word to begin a venture of his own — Success Motivation Institute.

SMI and its several offshoots were, and still are, service industries. Like all businesses, they depend on the provision of key investments (productivity, advertising, a good product, good customer relations) to achieve the desired return (enhanced reputation, sales).   Now that self-improvement has become so prominent a part of American culture, it is hard to imagine the revolutionary impact of Paul's ideas.   He was driven by an intense belief in the potential of every individual.   The pressures and routines of daily life, he felt, obscured vast stores of underutilized gifts — stores that could be retrieved by the application of certain disciplines and techniques.

The company started life in Paul's converted garage, where he and his first employee John Cook set up a two-man assembly line to put together SMI's original products, 33rpm record condensations of popular self-improvement books.   They arranged for a California firm to press the records. The marketing and shipping was done from Waco.   Appropriately enough, the first 500 records went to Zig Zigler.   Three years later Paul produced his own complete self-improvement and goal-setting programs, supplementing the records with printed scripts and a portable, battery-operated record player for use in a car.   The package was called *Your Personal Success Planner*.   Paul never looked back.

I still have one of those courses, which I highly valued even though I did not know Paul Meyer.   Eleven years went by before I met the man whose materials have done so much to benefit American society.

1. Know that everybody matters

Around the turn of the twentieth century public opinion about philanthropy began to change.   As George Bernard Shaw put it in his

Paul's Waco employee annual meeting. "If people aren't exploited, unions aren't necessary."

Socialism for Millionaires (1896), "We often give to public objects money that we should devote to raising wages. . .or substituting three eight-hour shifts for two twelve-hour ones." People were coming around to the view that philanthropy should address not only the manner in which money was spent but also the manner in which it was earned. The big-time givers should first put their own houses in order.

Paul Meyer applies the rule stringently. In his business philosophy, he puts the profit motive to the rear, key relationships to the fore.

"I don't have a goal to see how big I can get," he says. "All of our companies are small companies. Most people get caught up, and they want to be on the Fortune 500 list. I don't want to get big. All I want to do is make sure that our Meyer family companies serve the customer, produce quality products, and pay the employees well. I put me last."

This gives Paul Meyer an affinity to Rich DeVos, who argues in *Compassionate Capitalism* that the cultivation of compassionate attitudes and behavior patterns in the marketplace identify "the secret to real financial success." In DeVos's view, "we need to ask ourselves daily: 'How compassionate am I in caring for my coworkers, my supervisor, my employer or my employees, my suppliers, my customers, and even my competitors and what difference does it make?'"[19]

In his book DeVos defends the idea that noneconomic investments are economically valuable. What he calls compassionate capitalism *does* make a difference, because relationships comprise a key resource, and the wise manager will cultivate them by treating his people with respect. For that reason, and unusual for a corporate boss, Paul Meyer shows a high sensitivity to overworking among his staff.

"One of my managers has a powerful work ethic. I have to keep taking the pressure off her production. I say, 'Hey, look. Your personal life — your relationship with your husband and family — is more important than getting my work done. The work's going to happen. If everything you think you are going to get done in 30 days takes 60 days, it's okay with me. Why do I say that? Because I'm selfish. I want my people to be productive, but positively productive, with high quality. And also I want the work to endure."

Abuse of employees in industry angers and amazes him.

"Modern business is all about 'I'm going to get you before you get me.' And the employees are expendable, usable. That's been my observation with most companies I've seen. It's hideous. And they are building on quicksand. That's the reason we have all the problems. I mean, can you imagine my employees wanting to form a union? Somebody said to me once, 'Aren't you afraid of unions?' And I said, 'What?' The only reason a union was ever started was because of corruption in ownership and management. If people weren't exploited, unions wouldn't be necessary.

"And look at the downstream costs of exploitation. I was down in San Salvador one time, about fifteen years ago. And I was just asking questions. I said, 'How much do these workers make?' My informant said, 'A dollar a day.' And I said, 'If you keep doing that, one day they are going to get together and say they've had enough. And then they are going to walk right over you. They'll kill you, and kill your families, and you are going to have a war down here that you can't even imagine.' And I snapped my fingers twice, and it's happening. They've got trouble. Why? Because they exploited people. And company after company after company after company in America does that same thing right now."

Paul's belief in human potential always leads him to believe the best of others. He gives others the chance to achieve their goals, or to take on an assignment or an opportunity. He does not label people, or decide in advance that a particular individual is incapable of performing a particular task.

Inevitably a fallout occurs. Periodically staff fail, sometimes disastrously. But here Paul responds very differently from the average company executive. Failure doesn't lead automatically to dismissal.

"I don't fire people when they don't do a good job. If a person isn't performing well, I get some other people together and form a committee. I say 'We're not going to fire you. We're going to give you this support. You can borrow this brain power until you can get back on track. When you get back on track, then they will disband and leave you on your own again.' I don't know why more companies don't do that. They will fire a person who has made *one* mistake, when he's doing ninety percent a good job.

"For example, about two years ago I asked one of our top executives who had a big financial problem, 'Why didn't you say something? One skill I've got is solving problems — that's like shooting fish in a rain barrel for me. Why didn't you just tell me about it?'

"So finally he did. He thought he was going to get fired. I told him, 'I'm not going to fire you. You just made some lousy investments. People like me who live in a glass house can't throw rocks. Let me show you how to solve your problem.' So I called a colleague, L.D.Tanner, and we took this man's problem apart, and everything fell into place — we sorted it all out for him, and got him back on track financially."

In his early days as a sales manager, Paul employed less gentle methods. If a sales person came into Paul's office wanting a shoulder to cry on, he'd open a drawer and produce an axe. "Let me cut off your hand here," he'd say, placing a finger on your wrist. "That way you can use my hand. Seeing as you won't use yours." Other props included a box of pablum ("Only cry-babies want everything ready-chewed for them") and a back-brace ("Put this on and see if it'll help"). Paul would say any time you let others do for you that which you should do for yourself, they make you a lesser person.

Time has mellowed him. Every one of his employees knows

that Paul Meyer cares more about their families than he does about his business. And it makes them fiercely loyal.

"There's a powerful pay-back," says Paul. "I hardly ever lose anybody who works for me. Many of my key people have been with me over twenty years. I've got loyalty like I've never seen before.

"For example, Gladys Hudson, who is president of Passport to Success Foundation, flew to Florida several years ago to have an operation to remove cataracts and do a lens implant. I got to thinking about her flying all that distance home on the day after surgery and being exposed to no telling what kind of infection in a big crowded airport and plane. So I called her hotel and asked, 'Are you planning to fly home today?'

"'In about three hours,' she replied.

"'Well, just drive out to the airport. I'm sending my Lear jet to pick you up. You'll be home in half the time.'

"She was so stunned, she didn't say anything for a minute, and then started crying on the telephone. Any time I can make life better for an employee, I do it. Gladys Hudson would work day and night for me. So I feel like I can never pay her enough. And I feel that way about all of them. Anytime I can make life better for an employee, I do it. It makes a neat deal for me, because when I go away they run the business better than I can run it. They watch the money better than I can watch it. They come up with better ideas."

2. Know that you give to win

Paul Meyer believes in what he calls "core values."

"It's my view," he says, "that young people on a fast track often suffer from selfishness, self-centeredness, greed, and blind ambition. They have a rationalized, distorted value system — situational ethics. My core values haven't changed a lot because they are just that — core values that are ingrained at the core of my inner being." That he had lost sight of these values in his early twenties is one reason Paul remains thankful for the disaster at National Union. "After that I made a giant step back to these core values. Since then I think I've been making steady progress in improving my values."

But at a purely commercial level, are values *good* for business? It's a hotly debated topic.

When Philippe Kahn started the computer software company

Borland International, he faced an almost insurmountable problem. He needed to place an advertisement in *BYTE* magazine. Of all the microcomputer magazines, only *BYTE* catered to programmers, Kahn's key market. But he couldn't afford an ad, and the only way to get it was to convince *BYTE* to extend credit terms. He told the story to *Inc* as follows:

> What we did was, before the ad salesman came in — we existed in two small rooms, but I had hired extra people so we would look like a busy, venture-backed company — we prepared a chart with what we pretended was our media plan for the computer magazines. On the chart we had BYTE crossed out. When the salesman arrived, we made sure the phones were ringing and the extras were scurrying around. Here was this chart he thought he wasn't supposed to see, so I pushed it out of the way. He said, "Hold on, can we get you in BYTE?" I said, "We don't really want to be in your book, it's not the right audience for us." "You've got to try," he pleaded. I said, "Frankly, our media plan is done, and we can't afford it." So he offered good terms, if only we'd let him run it just once. We expected we'd sell maybe $20,000 worth of software and at least pay for the ad. We sold $125,000 worth. Looking back now it's a funny story; then it was a big risk.[20]

The *Inc* interview was later quoted by two Harvard professors, Amar Bhide and Howard H.Stevenson, in an analysis of business ethics for the *Harvard Business Review*. Their conclusion: contrary to popular opinion, dishonesty pays.

I believe their conclusions to be false, but their arguments bear examination. In the marketplace, they argue, we go on giving through honesty and trust, not because such investments are financially rewarding (that, according to Bhide and Stevenson, is a myth), but because "we want to believe in ourselves and have others respect and believe in us. . .We keep promises because it is right to do so, not because it is good business."[21]

At first, they say, "These findings distressed us.. . . Surely that wasn't right or efficient, and the system needed to be fixed!"[22] But later they decided this situation created two big advantages. First, the fact that goodness comes hard actually raises its value, rather as the difficulty of climbing Everest makes its conquest a real accomplishment. If the opposite were true — if virtue were always rewarded and wrongdoing always punished — one could hardly be commended for choosing virtue: not to do so would be plain stupid.

Second, they argue, the fact that wrongdoing *is* often rewarded actually opens up an important margin for risk-taking and innovation which would be excluded in a system where only the honest dealers made a profit. How else would Kahn have gotten his company off the ground, if not by deceit? Without actually endorsing Kahn's strategy, then, Bhide and Stevenson suggest that it is advantageous to society at large that the system make room for such strategies to be used.

Once again, I disagree. Nevertheless, Bhide and Stevenson feel fortunate to live in a world of "trusting optimists who readily do business with strangers and innovators. A 26-year-old Steve Jobs with no track record to speak of or a 52-year-old Ray Kroc with nearly ten failures behind him can get support to start an Apple or a McDonald's . . . even unreconstructed scoundrels are tolerated in our world as long as they have something else to offer."[23]

At first sight these conclusions might seem to subvert any argument we might put forward for that particular form of giving we call "business ethics." Why be honest if honesty doesn't pay? Yet if you look closely you will see a contradiction here. Even Bhide and Stevenson concede that ethical behavior *does* pay. You act ethically to safeguard your reputation just as you act ethically to make a profit; the only difference lies in the nature of the return — you seek a relational return rather than a financial one.

It may be true, as Bhide and Stevenson claim, that the benefits of treachery are more immediate and tangible than those of loyalty. But the real issue isn't whether people profit financially by playing fast and loose (clearly they do and always have done), or even whether playing fast and loose can prove more lucrative than playing by the rules. *It's whether playing by the rules is in itself rewarding as well as right.* If playing by the rules *doesn't prove* rewarding — if ethical business people go bankrupt, and if a good reputation actually counts for nothing — then we might as well forget ethics altogether.

Figure 8.1 shows the problem as a set of quadrants. It's relatively easy to show what's going on in quadrants B and C. Watch a promotional video put out by Imperial Oil, and you will hear CEO Arden Haynes urging that "In all its actions, Imperial Oil

	PROFITABLE	UNPROFITABLE
ETHICAL	(A) Enlightened self-interest	(B) Self-sacrifice
UNETHICAL	Narrow self-interest (C)	Folly (D)

Figure 8.1: The business ethic quadrants

is dedicated to the principle of ethical leadership." Over the long view, claims Haynes "ethics is *never* bad business." Yet at least in the short-term the adoption of a moral stand can be costly. Interviewed by *Saturday Night* in 1990, Haynes conceded that "there are certain partnerships and kinds of businesses that we have decided not to go into because we didn't like the nature of the business." Declining to name names, he added that the declined opportunities "could have been highly beneficial."

"You turned down long-term benefits?" asked the interviewer. Haynes replied, "Sure."[24]

Quadrant C can be amply illustrated not just from the boardroom, as Bhide and Stevenson show, but also from the ordinary world of the employee. For instance, a survey recently run by *Working Woman* showed that "Readers considered stealing time (in the form of phony sick days or personal phone calls) and supplies (computer software, office staples) or sharing company discounts with outsiders only minor violations. And trading competitive information with friends in the same industry is OK with almost half the respondents. More than 60 percent would use a stolen secret report from a competitor's company."[25]

But the most interesting areas are quadrants A and D.

It is tempting to wax moralistic about quadrant D. Exxon and seven other oil companies persuaded the town of Valdez to accept a tanker terminal, claiming that a major spill was "highly unlikely." Their 1,800-page contingency plan ensured that any spill would be controlled within hours. Yet when Exxon's supertanker released over 240,000 barrels of oil, the promised equipment simply wasn't available. Result: an expensive disaster. Exxon's total costs may exceed $2 billion, compounded by severe restrictions imposed on its operations in Alaska.

Negligence justly punished, you might say. Yet the problem with a moralistic analysis of this kind is that the decision-making behind the disaster represented realistic risk-taking. The oil companies skimped on the cleanup hardware precisely because they believed a spill to be unlikely. Had the Exxon Valdez never gotten into trouble, such economies might well have been applauded as sound policy.

Bhide and Stevenson quote this example as the exception that proves the rule. Probably thousands of companies take comparable risks, and most of them get away with it. Generally, unethical behavior pays; nobody places himself deliberately in quadrant D. They all assume they are positioned in quadrant C, where unethical practices boost the profit margin. Only unforeseen mishaps push them across the line to the place where unethical behavior gets its just deserts. So certain is it, in fact, that wrongdoers usually benefit from their wrongdoing, that a foundation for good behavior in simple moral conviction seems alarmingly fragile. What if all the good people in the world suddenly wised up and dismissed morality as an inconvenient nuisance?

The answer lies in reasons we examined earlier; sound business practice actually belongs in quadrant A. When faced with claims of product tampering, for instance, Johnson and Johnson immediately took Tylenol, its pain reliever, off the market. They knew the decision would cost heavily short-term, but they calculated that the greater cost lay in the loss of integrity. Their sales dropped dramatically, but the company, nevertheless ended up reinforcing its strong market leadership. You must remember also that, unlike Exxon, Johnson and Johnson, had not indulged in speculation; someone else had tampered with Tylenol.

No less an authority than management guru Peter Drucker has emphasized the need for corporate leaders to examine the real foundations of self-interest:

> Their own self-interest forces them to be concerned with society and community and to be prepared to shoulder responsibility beyond their own main areas of task and

responsibility. But, in doing this, they have to be conscious of the danger — to themselves and to society. They have to be conscious of the risk. No pluralist society has ever worked unless its key institutions take responsibility for the common good.[26]

This recognition has fueled the recent popularity of the term "stakeholder" in describing the varied interests surrounding the operation of a particular company. Such interests do not necessarily coincide: "In reality, shareholders want higher profits, customers want lower prices, labor wants better wages. As for the community, the philosopher Michael Yoe has aptly said that 'the question becomes whether what is good for General Motors is also and necessarily good for the nation.'"[27]

Divergent interests are notoriously hard to reconcile. But that's a problem for social theorists to worry about. What matters for the individual business person derives from the truth that ethical behavior pays in both relational and financial terms. It's "safe" to conduct business ethically, just as it's "safe" to practice philanthropy. God has so constructed the world that in the long run those who give don't lose out. They win. In fact it's a win-win situation. For everybody.

9

THE GIVER WHO MULTIPLIES
GIVING

T he easiest thing for people who have some money," says Paul Meyer, "is to write a check."

It bothers Paul to write checks. Don't get me wrong: he likes nothing better than to see needs being met. But in his heart of hearts he yearns to apply the resources as well as generate them. As he says, "Jane and I would rather put the band-aids on personally."

In this way he underlines the vital importance of the relationship between people who give and people who receive. But there is another key relationship involved in giving: the relationship between a philanthropist and that vast pool of individuals who have yet to discover and cultivate the art of good giving. Paul Meyer wants to *multiply* his stewardship.

Give more than money

For more than 40 years, Evelyn Collins ran a day-care center in an impoverished section of northwest Portland. It served 50 children of the area's working mothers. But hit by periodic cash shortages, the center had difficulty at times in paying its employees. And now the IRS was demanding $25,000 in unpaid taxes. The only option: closure.[28]

Collins — a woman in her late 70's — owes the salvation of the center to a local businessman, Robert Pamplin Jr. Pamplin paid most of the back taxes, and also gave Collins extra cash to fix up the center. But that wasn't the only or even the most important thing he did.

"What she really needed was not just the money," he recalled later, "but someone who could go to the IRS for her and straighten things out."

That's exactly what Pamplin did, using his reputation as a Forbes Four Hundred member and Christian minister to persuade

More than money. Paul's property Summer's Mill houses his classic car collection, and is used regularly for charitable work.

local IRS officials that Collins had not intended to cheat the government. He also worked out a fresh repayment schedule. The application of his business skill kept the center on the Portland map.

For Pamplin, this expressed a life philosophy. "Business people," he says, "have to take the entrepreneurial spirit that they applied to business and apply it to charity. That's what real charity is all about. I'm trying to show that this can be done creatively and successfully."

Pamplin has been pushing this idea for a long time. In 1971, at the age of 30, he pulled the University of Portland from financial ruin. He donated $450,000, helped raise a matching sum from other donors, and, most importantly, assisted the university in restructuring its finances. The University has kept him on as financial advisor; it has never again been in the red.

In arguing that business people can give their expertise as well as their cash, Pamplin vindicates a key principle. Any resource can be given, not only finance. Many of us employ this tactic directly. For instance, we may lend a hand to the Little League baseball club. But we can also, and perhaps more usefully, lend our specialized knowledge (think of the possibilities: accounting, computing, marketing, writing, chess). We can give our creativity, ideas, and experience. And we can give our relationships and contacts by bringing together somebody who needs help with somebody else who's willing and able to supply it.

Paul Meyer calls this "intelligence outside yourself."

The stewardship multiplier

Paul Meyer will often give his time/energy in the form of the services of an executive staff member. It's a powerfully effective strategy. He explains the reasoning behind it.

"Take a city with approximately 140,000 people. Suppose the top hundred companies in that town had their top five people, male or female, spend 15 to 25 percent of their company time working in local charities, service organizations, or ministries. That would be 500 people. What would happen in that city? Think of the change of tone, of climate, of attitude. And what kind of percentages would you get? It would be incalculable, unbelievable. That's why I encourage my top executives to work for charity while they're on my payroll."

The list is impressive.

For over fifteen years, Charles G. ("Chuck") Williams has spent between an hour and two hours a day of his executive time working for the Heart of Texas Council of Scouts — the premier scout organization in the United States. In Paul Meyer's judgment, Williams has put more time into the scouts than any voluntary contributor. A powerful catalyst, he gave the Heart of Texas Council of Scouts an incredible goals program. He raised the number of scouts from 4,000 to 7,000. He is "Mr. Boy Scouts of Central Texas," always behind the scenes, yet always giving recognition to other people. Paul Meyer also describes Chuck (a highly valued prayer partner and a colleague of 25 years) as the best Sunday School teacher he's ever heard and an outstanding preacher.

Gladys Hudson, previously the president of Paul's Product Development Company, is the immediate past president of the Waco YWCA and gave 25 percent of company time for two years to the construction of new YWCA facilities in Waco. The new building — rated among the finest in Texas — would not exist but for her input. Her position as president of Paul's Passport to Success Program has given that ministry its own special character. Hudson goes on television to promote it several times a year, writes a weekly column

*Jane Meyer gives out diplomas to the child "graduates" of the
LaRue Learning Center -- a preschool program supported by Paul.*

about it in the newspaper.   She has personally appointed the
administrative head and the development director. She has developed
all the brochures and materials.

The fact that a small city like Waco boasts three Boys and Girls
Clubs (not even Dallas has three), and that in several programs these
rank among the top of the 1,100 clubs spread across the United
States, owes much to the dedication of Gene Franklin and L.D.
Tanner. They've gone over every detail of the plans for the buildings,
raised large sums in funding. For two decades they gave the clubs
between 10 and 20 percent of their company time. L.D. Tanner —
once vice-president in charge of the region west of the Mississippi
for New York's Beneficial Finance — spends a full 25 percent of his
time at night working on a special needs ministry for the Meyer
family. He goes out and interviews people, checks on them. He has

Paul and Jane with President George Bush at the 1994 Boy Scouts Distinguished Citizen Award. Paul urges his executives to assist charity organizations on their company time.

a four-drawer file cabinet for his information on all these people. He's 75 years old, but he thinks, acts, and walks like he's 60 years old.

There are many more.

Barbara Chesser, Ph.D., majors on helping Paul with the Success Club and his One-on-One Special Needs ministry, and also helps Jane with the LaRue Learning Center and Gladys Hudson with Passport to Success.

Rose Frost and her staff handle all of Paul's money for charity. Rose keeps up with all of the details, and enjoys Paul's complete confidence. In the 90 days before I talked with her, she'd closed fifteen loans.

Bill Hinson stays in constant touch with people at over twenty ministries, including Angel House, the Community Training Center in East Waco, the Boy Scouts, and the Boys and Girls Clubs. "When he's out there," says Paul, "I feel that a piece of me is out there."

Ferrell Hunter, Paul Meyer's in-house consultant, helps to free up other people's time by watching over more than fifteen of Paul's companies as CEO. "In over fifteen companies," Paul says, "he gives me the best advice."

Gene Franklyn does anything and everything — helping with the Boys and Girls Clubs, auditing the Family Foundation's books — and never asks for a word of thanks.

Space does not permit me to eulogize about Paul's trusted and experienced colleague Joe Baxter, or a dozen others who take part in, and multiply, Paul Meyer's giving.

They testify to a deliberate strategy. Paul's rule for his executives is, "charitable organizations first, business second." Says Paul, "I want to use my testimony to motivate other people to do a better job with stewardship. I would like to sell the business community on being less selfish. We can't just take, take, take from the world of business. We need to give back. And I'd like to tell the business community, 'If you take your top 25 percent of your executives and let them work in charity, they're going to do more work on the job than they do now.' I would like to influence people not only to give their money and time, but to give their people's time. My best multiplier consists of the top 20 executives in our company."

Do you want a multiplier? I'm looking for a multiplier for Paul Meyer.

10

THE GIVER WHO LOVES TO GIVE

On Sunday, February 2, 1992, Paul Meyer sat down at his desk and wrote a letter to his youngest daughter Leslie. "Leslie," he began:

> *We all run into walls, obstacles, people who think differently or have a different view or perspective. How we act or react can have positive or negative effects on our lives.*
>
> *It's not what happens to us that matters, but rather, our attitude toward what happens. . . .*
>
> *Leslie — if someone hurts you by something they have said or something they have done — then you take the initiate to clear it up. . . .*
>
> *Then renew your relationship — your commitment to the thing you have in common, that you enjoy participating in together, that unites you as friends. Differences aren't erased or ignored; they are put on the back shelf — the issue of proving who's right or wrong is never, never, never as important as the relationship.*

The full text of the letter can be found in Appendix 2. Paul Meyer's advice to his daughter gives a unique insight into the man who is without doubt America's most creative, prolific, and dedicated giver. Naturally, it condenses a lifetime of experience. But it also reflects his commitment to what he calls the "total person," and what others commonly idealize as a "balanced life."

Remarkably few people, though, achieve anything like a satisfactory balance. How often have you heard somebody complain that "there just aren't enough hours in the day," or say "I'd like to do such and such, but I simply don't have the time"? They fail to translate their time/energy evenly into the other resources. One or two resources receive the bulk of their attention, and the rest go by the board.

You find the classic example of this in a man's need to juggle the demands of his work and his home. Often he will put so much time/energy into his work that he fails to care for his family relationships. He comes home late; he's tired; and he has nothing left to give his wife and children. He also has nothing left for his intellect, because he's too physically and mentally exhausted to pick up a book. So he turns on the television set to watch a sports event which demands neither physical exertion nor mental concentration. He certainly has no resources left for his body or spirit. Everything goes into making money.

Well, making money is important. But if you let the demands of the workplace drain your other resources you will set a less than optimum limit on your earnings.

"There's a man I've known a long, long time," says Paul Meyer. "I helped motivate him to go through law school, and he said the other day he was just working hard and feeling trapped.

"So I gave him two articles about being trapped. I gave him a tape — a talk I made last year about being a total person and living a balanced life. Then I wrote him a letter about how his priorities should be God first, his wife and children second, and third having a good time and going hunting with his friend or playing golf or whatever he wants to do. His law practice should come about fifth. If he keeps it there, he's going to have more business than he can handle. He'll make more money than he's making now. And he'll have more success than he has now."

By balancing and prioritizing correctly?

"Absolutely. For one thing, he's going to get rid of the stress in his life, get rid of the anxiety, get rid of the tension."

Paul himself always puts relationships first: he knows how vital they are. He also knows how voraciously a business can devour his time. Consequently, he enshrines his priorities in his planning.

"Jane and I plan what we're going to do with our family at the beginning of the year. That's first, and everything else comes in second. That's important to us. Business could consume all the time I have. If we didn't put family time first, we wouldn't have it."

Relationships mean more than just family. Melinda Cochran's husband had worked for Paul eighteen years when they were divorced. Melinda had been a school teacher but had contracted multiple sclerosis. She moved to San Francisco where doctors thought the climate would be better for her. She decided she needed to go back to school to prepare for a career she could manage with her physical limitations, but she did not have the funds necessary and had not been living in California long enough to qualify for state rehabilitation funds. Paul Meyer heard of her plight and stepped in with the help she needed. He gave her a scholarship to study counseling and international relations. She is now completing her Ph.D. and is experiencing success as a counselor. Her physical condition has continued to deteriorate, and she is wheelchair bound and must have assistance for personal care. But she has found the courage to persist in her studies and her career largely because Paul's help gave her a jump-start back to belief in her competence.

For Paul, virtually nothing stands in the way of meeting another's personal need.

"I'll phone in and cancel a meeting if somebody calls me and wants some help. I put that first, and I put business second. The business is always going to be there. There's enough business to work 24 hours a day the rest of your life, and you wouldn't put a dent in it."

Of course the reverse also applies. Paul directs so much of his energy to meeting needs that one wonders how he stops philanthropy crowding out his work. He explains it with a smile. "Well, I find my adrenalin's pumping higher, and I produce more in the time I have left than I would by giving business my whole day."

Balancing the different areas of your life doesn't mean distributing your time/energy equally between them. For one thing, you can feed two life-areas at the same time. Work in the construction industry, or some other outdoor occupation, and you will build your physical resources while you earn your money. Find a job that's challenging and stimulating, and you will feed your intellect as you sit at your desk. Some people enjoy solitude because it builds their inner resources and creativity; others seek out company, work out or engage in debate with friends because they want to develop their relationships. Specifically, I have a friend who engages in extra prayer during his sixty-minute morning walk.

Also, different areas of life demand different kinds and degrees of attention. Finance tends to remain a permanent factor, in the sense that most employed people devote a certain number of hours each week to their job. Similarly, the value of interaction with others increases steeply on special occasions: meals, for instance, or Saturday drives, or shared family devotions. And both finance and relationships will usually take up more time/energy than physical exercise. Keeping fit requires only a daily half hour in the fitness center — or a bicycle ride to the store.

As for your spiritual needs, many people will recommend spending time in devotions early in the morning, before the distractions of the day begin. Yet giving in spirituality, like giving in relationships, isn't only a matter of how much time/energy you allocate. It's also about the values which govern your behavior. When Paul Meyer talks about "putting God first" he doesn't mean he's spending sunup to sundown on his knees. God enters into every aspect of his life.

"It is imperative," Paul Meyer wrote to Leslie,

> *that we choose a proactive or positive response. Choosing forces us to gain perspective and then decide our own actions or reaction. Choosing is accepting responsibility for our attitude and action. Choosing a proactive response to what people say or do is the only way to live life without blaming others or circumstance.*
>
> *Unless we choose, or exercise the power to choose, our actions & behavior will be determined by conditions or what other people say, think, or do.*

Look at the way Paul Meyer lives his life and you will distill six principles to help you develop giving values.

1. Make giving your philosophy

Paul Meyer learned about giving when a lad. He wasn't raised on easy street. Of limited means, his parents had first set up housekeeping in a tent in California's Santa Clara Valley. They expected Paul, the youngest of three children, to pull his weight.

If he wanted something, he had to earn it. And at age fourteen, one overriding desire dominated his thinking. He passionately wanted an $85 racing bike he'd seen in a sports store window in San Jose. He worked himself into the ground to get that bike. He broke national records selling copies of *Liberty Magazine* and *Ladies Home Journal*. He employed forty of his friends to pick California prunes

— persuading the orchard owner to pay him by the box. He hired helpers on a commission basis. He made a five-cent override on their work. In the end, because he was so worried the shop owner would sell the bike before he could earn his $85, he borrowed the shortfall from his mother.

In today's money that bicycle would cost about $1,500. Every imaginable accessory had been attached: lights, saddlebags, basket, reflectors. For years Paul Meyer had yearned to own a bike like this. Now he had it. Riding back from the bakery with day-old bread, melon, and powdered potatoes for his mother, he felt like the richest person in town.

But he didn't keep it long.

The year was 1941. The Japanese had just attacked Pearl Harbor, forcing the United States into war. These events held special significance for the young Paul Meyer, for a Japanese-American boy in the town where the Meyers lived happened to be his best friend. Shortly after Paul bought the bicycle, the news broke that the United States government would intern Japanese-Americans. Realizing he might not see his friend again, Paul Meyer went straight over to his house — and gave him the bike.

Talk to Paul Meyer today and you will find that this simple selfless act has flowered into a whole philosophy of life.

"I just think that if people would forget about the getting, just give, give, give, give, give, give — that's the only way they're going to have peace and joy. That's what I've spent a lifetime doing. I do a little better job at it each year. But I'm still far short of what I would like to be. I'm afraid time is running out on me. I'm going to die before I can even make a dent in it."

He has even taken the unusual step of committing this philosophy to writing. "My entire goals program has a spiritual foundation," he explains. "It is anchored in my relationship with Jesus Christ and my dependence on God. In the process of crystallizing my thinking about my goals, I developed a five-point Philosophy of Living that serves as a set of criteria for evaluating all the goals I have ever set in every area of life."

The five points are these:

1.   A POSITIVE ATTITUDE.

I have a positive attitude. I was taught that the glass is half full and not half empty — to live with positive expectation. The basis of this attitude comes from. . .

Philippians 2:5 — "Let this mind be in you which was also in Christ Jesus."

2. NO WORRY.
    I thank God I am not a worrier. Worry dilutes my strength and diminishes my ability to produce or to be effective. The scripture gives us the best instruction and affirmation in the following. . .

    Philippians 4:6-7 — "Be anxious for nothing, but in everything in prayer and supplication with thanksgiving, let your requests be made known to God; and the peace of God, which surpasses all understanding, will guard your hearts and minds through Christ Jesus."

3. PEACE AND CONTENTMENT.
    I am happy every day because it is a day that God has given me. Since He has given it to me, it is good. I know that all sunshine makes a desert. I know that there are always changes — some good, some bad, some up, and some down. I have learned to have peace and contentment regardless of what state I am in. Again, this was given to me from God's word in. . .

    Philippians 4:11 — "Not that I speak in regard to need, for I have learned in whatever state I am, to be content."

4. STRENGTH AND POWER TO ACHIEVE.
    I see myself as an entrepreneur, a risk-taker, courageous, bold, aggressive, and willing to attempt new ideas and seek new paths — and why not? My potential to achieve is backed by the power of Christ. I know if I seek His will that He is my constant companion and partner and He gives me strength and power to achieve which comes from. . .

    Philippians 4:13 — "I can do all things through Christ who strengthens me."

5. STEWARDSHIP.
    Obviously everything belongs to God by right of creation. Out

of His love for me, He has let me use some of His riches. Because I have committed my life to Christ and put Him on the throne of my life and have put Him in control, I know that I do what I do because of Him, and that I achieve what I achieve because of Him. The greatest joys and pleasures of my life are giving and sharing.

Financial stewardship is the only subject mentioned in the Bible where God said to test him in tithing and giving. If you give back to Him, He will pour out a blessing that you do not have room enough to hold. My affirmation for this comes from. . .

Luke 6:38 — "Give, and it will be given to you; good measure, pressed down, shaken together, and running over will be put into your bosom. For with the same measure that you use, it will be measured back to you."

Paul concludes by saying, "I believe that every person should have a Philosophy of Living, and I am a strong believer in writing things down. Writing crystallizes thought — writing forces you to think out your ideas clearly. Clear thinking motivates positive action. Your philosophy of life may be partially like mine or nothing like mine, but it should express your uniqueness and should reflect your relationship to God, and be a pattern for your Christian lifestyle."

They don't teach values like Paul Meyer's at the business schools.   "It's a hard sell," admits Paul. "If you go to the University of Michigan, Harvard Business School, Stanford University, the University of Texas — what do they teach you there? It's how to climb the corporate ladder, how to get on top. And everybody gets in that dumb race. Their values — if they had any — get compromised."

He openly blames ignorance about the principles of giving for business failure. "I think if we have a downfall with our business, if we get in second place, it's because of greed and selfishness and self-centeredness. We get off track. We forget the purpose of being in business. The only purpose for being in business is to serve. The only reason to be alive is to serve."

Yet it takes time to make giving your normal paradigm. The

value-system behind it has to be worked at, internalized, imprinted on the mind through practice. Put it another way: giving has to become a habit. We should reach a point where we don't think about it any more, just do it. And that requires an investment of time/energy, just like driving a car. At first you have to think everything out, consciously coordinate your movements, force your hands and feet to do what feels unnatural to them. Only with practice does driving become second nature and gradually yield a new and greater freedom.

The learning may be slow. We don't easily shake off the "collection plate" mentality, the fear that giving will prove to be a zero-sum game where our resources are sacrificed to the needs of others. But we should persevere, because habitual giving lies at the heart of philanthropy.

The author Miranda Seymour, for example, recalls visiting a fellow writer, famed for the quality of his library:

> We were talking about the typical bibliophiles's hatred of people who borrow books surreptitiously and never give them back. The writer found this resentment utterly baffling. "But I love it when people take my books away," he said. "They obviously want to read them, and they leave me with the space for new ones!" That's what I call a truly generous nature.[29]

2. See what will be, not what is

Paul Meyer launched Success Motivation Institute in a converted garage. You could not describe it as spacious or inspiring. Paul knew that if he sat at his desk and looked at that garage long enough, he would see it for what it was: a converted garage. So he hired an architect, and told him to draw up an impression of the building Paul hoped his company would one day occupy.

Visualization means seeing something not as it is, but as it *will* be. Paul used the same technique in selling. If a prospect possessed only a J.C. Penny suit, Paul would take him to a tailor, dress him up in a suit he couldn't afford, then whip out a polaroid and take a picture. If a prospect drove a junk car, Paul would take him to the showroom and photograph him in a Cadillac. If a prospect lived in a house trailer, Paul showed took him through a three-bedroom, two-bath brick, and got out the camera. Whatever the prospect most desired, Paul put it on film.

Of course you can also visualize mentally. During an early financial crisis, Norman Vincent Peale jammed his *Guideposts* magazine's numerous unpaid bills onto a spike, and set the spike down in the middle of the directors' conference table. "Look at those bills," he said. He recalls that a deep silence fell on the room, until Tessie, a nondirector he'd co-opted for the occasion, took the meeting by the scruff of the neck and shook it.

"Let us examine the situation," she said. "You lack everything. You lack money, you lack subscribers, you lack equipment, you lack ideas. And why do you lack? Simply because you have constantly and consistently been thinking in terms of lack, and have thereby created a condition of lack."

She then pounced on Dr. Peale.

> "How many subscribers do you need to keep this magazine going?" she asked. I did not know for sure, but picked a figure at random and said that a hundred thousand would do it. "All right. What I want you to do is to look out there and see, visualize, imagine a hundred thousand people reading Guideposts who have paid for their subscriptions."
>
> As she said this I happened to look into her snapping brown eyes, and I was reminded of the exalted look of the believer. Tessie was not of my church. She was Jewish, a compelling combination of spirituality and sagacity. Mirrored in her eyes I "saw" the required hundred thousand subscribers. In excitement I leaped to my feet and shouted, "I see them, I see them."
>
> Tessie jumped up also and threw her arms round me. "Isn't that wonderful?" she exclaimed. "Now that we see them, we have them."

That might seem an exaggerated, or at least an optimistic, claim. However, Dr. Peale goes on:

> And that is precisely what happened in this instance. Our directors came alive and began to throw out ideas, one after the other. Of course some 90 percent of them were of no value. But 10 percent were very good ideas indeed. And as a result, those bills melted away.[30]

Visualization works because it bridges an unbridgeable gap. Until Tessie made the directors "see" their subscribers reading the magazine, a hundred thousand subscriptions was just so much ink on a sheet of paper, an impossible target that might as well have been a billion. Visualization brought the target close enough that it began to inspire real plans to reach it.

3. Remember who you are and what you're doing

Closely related to visualization, but distinct from it, is affirmation. Cynics sometimes caricature affirmation. But we should not lightly dismiss the psychology behind it. When we use an affirmation, we remind ourselves of who we are and what we are doing. Affirmation keeps us focused. People repeat affirmations regularly — perhaps early in the morning or last thing at night — because they want to spread this self-knowledge through the rhythms of daily life. They know how easily they get distracted and drift. They see the value of giving themselves a regular briefing to realign their daily program with their life goals.

At 70 years of age I reinforce my personal physical fitness program with at least twenty affirmations that remind me of the benefits physical fitness will bring me, physically, mentally, financially, relationally, and spiritually. By the time I've gone through those affirmations I have no trouble motivating myself to exercise. I know why I'm keeping fit. I want to do it.

Norman Vincent Peale's sermon pamphlets provided a potent source of affirmation for the young Paul Meyer. Today Paul more often uses Bible passages. In the front of his prayer journal you will find the words:

> I believe in the power of God; I have experienced Christ's
> saving power; I know His presence-power; and I daily claim
> His prayer power.

Ten Scripture verses follow. Paul has affirmations for every area of his life and work, and he interweaves them with his prayer. Before praying for his family he will say:

> I believe in God's family plan; I accept my spiritual role and responsibility as husband and father; I commit my family to God in daily prayer!

His affirmation on charities and ministries runs:

> I believe God has given me the gift of stewardship; I earn to give; I live to share; I multiply my personal ministry by giving in Jesus's name!

Paul doesn't put affirmations in his journal just to fill the pages. He is reminding himself daily of why he prays and what he seeks to accomplish.   Affirmations spring naturally from goals.   Prayer followed and undergirded by affirmation produces the power to act. It's a potent combination.   And it explains the energy with which Paul Meyer and his wife Jane both seek opportunities to give.   Every day they look for some special need to fill, something that will be overlooked if they don't act on it: paying for a nurse, reducing rent, underwriting an apartment for a foreign student, paying an air fare to let someone visit a dying relative.   Through affirmation, Paul Meyer frequently discovers that God accomplishes through Paul himself the answer to his own highly specific prayers.

4. Train yourself to think ahead.

Events unfold slowly.   The foundations of the next decade have already been laid; they were probably laid twenty years ago.   That gives you the clue to why some of the most spectacular economic success stories can be traced to long-term planning — for example, in Singapore, where policy objectives are set not for five years, but for twenty-five.

Ask Paul Meyer about his businesses.   "I plan ahead five to twenty years.   In some of our companies we have a detailed plan of the year 2010.   I have many, many businesses that we operated for ten years before they made a profit or turned the corner.

He names a specific company.   "When we took it over, it had suffered an 80 percent drop in sales due to being looted and raped by former management.   A lot of people would have left it to go bankrupt, but I choose to resurrect it because I see its potential over the next thirty years."

Almost everything in Paul's life appears geared to the long-term. He makes no secret of it. "When I passed my thirtieth birthday, I made the first major shift to long-range thinking, and every year since I do more of it. That's the reason I take care of myself physically," he says. "That is the reason I read and study. That is the reason I maintain friendships for a lifetime. It is the reason I save. It's a different lifestyle—a different outlook on life — when you think long-range. The biggest mistake made in American business is the lack of long-range thinking, and the lack of deployment of assets for long-range projects like research and development. Time and time again, American companies and individuals make short-term decisions which sacrifice the future just for a quarterly profit, or for a mention in the papers, or for fifty other reasons." He smiles. "I just view everything differently than 99 percent of the people that I know."

For Paul, one crucial aspect of long-range thinking is long-range commitment to relationships. He tends to go by his intuition. A few years ago he glanced at a brochure produced by Marketplace Ministries.

"Who designed this?" he asked. It turned out to be a student who had just graduated from Baylor, named Amy Hoekstra. Paul arranged an interview. He'd never hired anybody that young, right out of college. But her sharpness and maturity astounded him. She came on the payroll. Anxious to keep her, Paul offered her father, recently retired from the U.S. Air Force, a position with one of his companies, and moved the family to Waco.

"Really I was doing that selfishly, to please her. This girl has been offered deals at America's top universities. She can go anywhere she wants, and get anything she wants. She's that bright. But here's what happened to me. Her father is so sharp, he's better than anybody I could ever have found in a million years for the job he's on. I hit the jackpot."

5. Organize forwards and backwards.

Pundits describe Paul Meyer as one of the greatest closers of his generation. For example, the famous sales writer Charles B. Roth has written about Paul's genius in closing sales.

How does Paul explain his extraordinary success as a salesman? One thing is exhaustive preparation.

"I only see people who are Class A prospects and that I have been sent to see by people they respect. I ask a lot of questions of the person who gives me a prospect's name. Therefore I am fully armed with a psychological profile and needs survey."

He also achieves high levels of synergism. His clients become his friends. He loves to help them; they love to help him. When his company held a sales contest Paul wrote to his clients telling them about the contest and asking if they'd mind helping him share with others the same service he'd shared with them. The number of names he received astonished him. He won the contest, hands down. In fact he's won every contest he's entered since the age of twelve. He recognizes relationships, like information, as a resource.

Organization is one of Paul Meyer's hallmarks. He organizes forward in planning and preparation, and in the judicious combining of resources. And he organizes backwards by keeping meticulous records. Enter the storeroom next to his study and you'll find shelf upon shelf of three ring binders: Business Operations, Recruiting System, Marketing System, Financial Records, Sales Associate Training Program, Conference Guides, Development and Career Opportunity, BSS. What does BSS stand for?

"Something to do with business systems," replies Paul. He flips a page and immediately has the precise title. "Here it is. Business Success System."

He has a second storeroom the same size in another part of Waco. Sometimes on a Saturday he will drive there and sift the shelves, throwing unwanted materials down into the middle of the room to be taken away. But he throws out nothing vital. In a recent court case Paul was able to produce the actual thirty-year-old bank check to prove the communication came from the American National Bank of Chicago and not from a particular individual. His attorney almost passed out with surprise.

6. Don't kid yourself

Almost nothing comes easier than to pretend things are going well when they're going badly. Almost nothing comes easier than to pretend your record's perfect — to save face — when you know

Baylor University President Herbert Reynolds with Paul and Jane in November 1993 when they received the highest award bestowed by Baylor University -- the Alumnus Causa. One professor commented after an address by Paul: "It's the first time I've seen all the students stay to the end of a lecture."

you've messed up. We see pretence as a way of escape. And it traps us.

Paul Meyer talks about failure candidly. Recently he addressed a graduate class in international marketing and entrepreneurship at Baylor University.

"You know, Bill Hinson and I talked about it ahead of time. He said to me, 'What are you going to tell these students out here?' I said, 'I think most businessmen lecture in universities for an ego trip. They get pompous and kind of brag. That's my perception of people who speak at universities. But I think I'll go out there and tell them to take off their Sunday mask. If they will be truthful, so will I. Then I can really make a contribution.'"

In preparation Paul went through all his business files and dug out details on every enterprise he'd ever attempted. He was astonished to find that 65 percent of everything he'd ever done had fallen flat on its face. Only about 35 percent of his attempted enterprises flourished. He had complete lists: all the companies, all the ideas — the ones that succeeded, and the ones that didn't.

"So I handed those out to the students. And I said, 'Let's ask some questions. Ask me anything you want about the businesses that prospered and the ones that didn't work. If they didn't work, ask me why.'"

It turned into a sensational event. Afterwards a head professor of the Baylor Business School told Paul it was the first time he'd seen all the students stay to the end of the lecture, the first time he'd seen them stay on afterwards, and the first time in five years he'd seen the students give the visiting speaker a standing ovation. And it was for lecturing on failure!

"I was really telling them," says Paul, "that if you're really going to do something with your life, you are going to fall down. You are going to fail. And there's nothing wrong with failing. To me, it's just one less mistake I'm going to make. It's a part of the education process."

And what about personal, as opposed to business, failure? Again, Paul's rule will not permit him to evade the issue. He refers to his pastor and lifelong friend, Bill Hinson.

"I feel like I owe him not to screw up. I owe him to live a Christlike life as much as possible. I want to be accountable to him as a Christian. I've got four or five friends like that. And I tell them, 'I want to be accountable to you, and if you see me off track, hear me say anything or do anything off track, or even hear of anything, I want you to tell me about it.' I think if everybody did that, we could keep from messing up a lot of things."

7. Enjoy!

"At length," wrote Charles Dickens in *A Christmas Carol*,

> the hour of shutting up the counting house arrived. With an ill-will Scrooge dismounted from his stool, and tacitly admitted the fact to the expectant clerk in his tank, who instantly snuffed his candle out, and put on his hat.
>
> "You'll want all day tomorrow, I suppose?" said Scrooge.
>
> "If it's quite convenient, sir."
>
> "It's not convenient," said Scrooge, "and it's not fair. If I was to stop half-a-crown for it, you'd think yourself ill-used, I'll be bound."

The clerk smiled faintly.

"And yet," said Scrooge, "you don't think me ill-used, when I pay a day's wages for no work."

The clerk observed that it was only once a year.

"A poor excuse for picking a man's pocket every twenty-fifth of December!" said Scrooge, buttoning his great-coat to the chin. "But I suppose you must have the whole day. Be here all the earlier next morning."

Scrooge portrays tightfistedness personified. He fears and resents every claim against his profit, symbolizing our natural tendency to think only in terms of returns. This amounts to an inhibition, a psychological knot that needs to be undone. We can only become givers if we realize that giving is "safe" — that it won't ruin us; that on the contrary it will build our success. Only this can release us from anxiety over finance and sweep away the tariff barriers of possessiveness to establish giving as a kind of "free trade" between the individual and society.

But when we follow this path we discover, almost incidentally, something very surprising: that giving is *fun.*

Darryl Johnson recalls that when he first went to Baylor University, he called Paul Meyer for the Boosters' Club to ask if he'd be willing to support a young person in need. Paul agreed. "But what I'll never forget," says Darryl, "is that before he hung up Paul *thanked* me for thinking of him, for letting him help." That's typical of Paul Meyer. He derives unspeakable joy from the practice of giving.

The cynic would argue that for many wealthy people the fun of giving lies in stroking their own egos. George Eastman said, "It is more fun to give money than to will it."[32] Another benefactor, Hugh Roy Cullen, chose to give away 90 percent of his estimated $200 million personal fortune before he died, "so that I may get a selfish pleasure out of spending it."[33] But one looks in vain for evidence of egotism in Paul Meyer. He speaks of his philanthropy as answering a personal "need," and constantly recommends giving as part of his philosophy of the happy life.

"When I find someone who is really unhappy and has a cantankerous attitude and is kind of a sourpuss, and they walk around that way, I say, 'If you want to shape up, start thinking about somebody else instead of yourself, and a complete transformation is going to take place in your life.'" He shrugs. "And it does."

Giving, then, quickly becomes what some would say it should never be: a source of intense gratification. Almost a thrill.

"I don't give to be paid back," says Paul. "That's what's hard for me to explain to people. I give because I have the need to give. I feel almost selfish. Like I helped two people on the airplane from Athens the other week. One was a woman who was having difficulty on the airplane. I helped her get a wheelchair and helped her around. And when I got through I sat there by myself in the airplane and thanked God that I was the one that got to help her."

On the same flight he met a stewardess. Seeing she was unhappy, he waited until everybody was asleep, then went forward and said, "Tell me about yourself."

She told him, "Well I've just had a bad operation. I've had some lymph nodes taken out and a mastectomy. They found out yesterday that I have cancer again."

Paul replied, "I can see it in your face. Has anybody else said anything to you about it?"

"No."

"Are you a Christian?"

"Yes."

Then Paul gave it to her straight. "Well, it doesn't make any difference then whether you live or die. Change your attitude. You need an abundant attitude whether you are well or sick. And if you have an abundant attitude you'll have a better shot at getting your health back."

She came to see him later when his wife had awakened, and said, "I can't believe that somebody I don't know would care about me."

Now he writes to her occasionally. "And I don't know this woman from Adam. But every morning I pray God will put somebody in front of me I can minister to that day, some way, somehow."

Recently Paul and Jane Meyer asked a young unmarried mother to their house. She'd never laid eyes on them before; they'd never laid eyes on her before. But someone had told the Meyers she needed help.

Paul said to her, "The first thing I heard was that you were going to buy shoes for your son, and you couldn't buy the shoes because you had to buy food instead. The second thing I heard was that you were tithing. I couldn't believe that a single mother with two children and no money for shoes would tithe her money first." Paul offered to have his own son, Jim, do the legal work for her to get money from her ex-husband. He then said he would give her a monthly check until she got back on her feet. "Before she went," he says, "we ran through the house and got a bunch of Leslie's and Jane's clothes for her, and got a bunch of my clothes for her sons. If they don't fit, I told her, bring them back so I can give them to somebody else. After she left I was high as a kite. I wished somebody else could come in after her, because that's the joy of giving. If I could, I'd give every moment of the day. That's the thrill of giving."

Eventually Scrooge learned that same thrill. Reformed by the visit of the famous ghosts, he "walked about the streets, and watched the people hurrying to and fro, and patted children on the head, and questioned beggars, and looked down into the kitchens of houses, and up to the windows, and found that everything could yield him pleasure. He had never dreamed that any walk — that anything — could give him so much happiness. . . . His own heart laughed, and that was quite enough for him."[34]

11

THE GIVER DEATH
WON'T STOP

T he child sits at a computer keyboard with earphones on. On the screen flashes the image of a golden retriever.

"Dog," says the computer. "D-o-g. Dog. Say dog."

"Dog," the child says.

"Now type 'dog.'"

The child types it, but incorrectly: d-o-t.

"Good try," says the computer. "Try again."

All the responses are positive. The child sees; the child hears; the child acts. The program works on all three of the ways people process information: visual, auditory, and kinesthetic. This is unusual. In the typical classroom, attention and praise focus on the students who learn by hearing and seeing. Students who learn kinesthetically — by doing — become marginalized and disadvantaged.

This software comes from one of Paul's companies: the Creative Education Institute. Does it work? Read a letter from Dabney Lessman, whose brother is on the program, and who, being a teenager, can be trusted not to pull her punches:

> *Dear Mr. Meyer,*
>
> *I wish you knew how much CEI has helped my younger brother Darrell. Before he started, my mom dreaded coming home. Every night, Sunday to Thursday, she had to stay up with Darrell until 11 or 12 at night. He might have a simple math problem like 576+891, and he would say he didn't know how to do it, and would ask for help, when he did know how to do it. In every single subject he asked for help, when really there was nothing that was too hard for him to do. He came up with some kind of excuse so he didn't have to do it himself. Several times I offered to show him how to figure it out on his own, but he only wanted someone to tell him the answers. Now Darrell does his homework on his own. He only asks for help on problems he really can't figure out. He's normally in bed by 9:30 or*

10. He really enjoys CEI. He told me so. It's amazing how much easier his homework is in four weeks. Just think how it'll be when he gets through! Thank you!!!!! You've made my whole family's life easier. Now my mom can bake cookies while my brother does his homework. She hasn't been able to do this for a long time.

Love in Christ,

Dabney Lessman.

In an accompanying letter, their mother, Donna, marvels at the transformation:

I don't really understand how CEI has brought about this change. Last year Darrell was frequently in the principal's office for not completing his work. The teacher called him "lazy" frequently, and on a couple of occasions "bad." Darrell is now one of the sweetest, hardest working boys I know. People at church compliment me frequently on having such sweet children. Darrell now tries his homework on his own; he is excited about learning. His reading has improved so very much — he's now reading a 200-page library book on his own. He really enjoys CEI and feels challenged by the point and prize system. I am free to spend more time with my daughter, and just doing mommy things. Before, every evening I would spend two or three hours trying to encourage Darrell to do his work. It was like trying to push a string. On occasion I would have to be more forceful than I care to be; now we can tease and play while doing homework. I love my children so much. Thank you for changing the world for me and my children.

CEO of the Creative Education Institute, Ferrell Hunter, sees the program that turned the Lessman home around as superior even to one-on-one teaching.

"Even if you have a one-to-one teacher ratio, you're still working with a tutorial concept that tries to get something into the child's head without correcting the weaknesses. The CEI approach is more therapeutic. You correct the child's weaknesses rather than just poking information. I know because I was in a project once to motivate adults returning to education. That's hard. This group of people went to school using books in classrooms and failed miserably, and 20 years later you're putting them back in another classroom with another set of books, and this time it's supposed to work. It's not going to work. You have to do something different with those people."

The CEI system gives the child a degree of control he doesn't have with an adult teacher. Hunter's convinced, because his own youngest grandson has used it.

"Going into first grade, he wasn't learning to read. He could say the alphabet but couldn't write it. It turned out when we tested him that he had zero visual memory. He could look up and see a letter, and by the time he looked down, he forgot what he saw. He's now in the third grade and doing very well."

The CEI program has met with phenomenal success. It's currently being used by over 800 school systems in Texas, and expanding all the time. Sales have doubled two years in a row. But this rapidly growing company might easily have gone under in the early years.

Joe Farrell, a former biology teacher, pioneered the system to overcome his son's severe learning difficulties. He started the company in 1987, but ran into financial trouble. Ferrell Hunter, a friend and consultant to Joe Farrell, suggested Joe allow Paul Meyer to buy him out. Paul purchased the company in 1991. Joe Farrell remains the president and inspiration of the company. Through Ferrell Hunter, Paul provides management and accounting expertise to back Joe Farrell up. Joe Farrell's son has now graduated from Baylor.

I tell this particular story because it illustrates well the thinking behind Paul's investment. He injected cash to rescue a fledgling company. But more than that, he gave financial stability to an educational service that will probably help hundreds of thousands of children. And he did it not by making a one-time donation but by setting up a self-sufficient, profit-making enterprise. His business not only supports socially beneficial activity; it is itself socially beneficial. Perhaps most significant, it will outlive him.

1. Pursue permanence

Lord Shaftesbury, the tireless campaigner for factory workers' rights in nineteenth-century Britain, once remarked, "When I feel age creeping upon me I am deeply grieved, for I cannot bear to go away and leave the world with so much misery in it."

It's worth asking what happens to your resources when you die. The answer may surprise you. Fairly obviously, you wipe out your store of time/energy: whether you get three score years and ten, or four or five score years, time/energy remains ever the finite resource. You can use it well or badly, save it or squander it, but either way, you cannot hoard it nor appreciably increase it.

By contrast, however, the other resources, the ones for which you exchange time/energy, may continue to work long after you have left the scene. In fact, they represent ways in which the individual can leave his or her indelible mark on history.

Think of information. "This is the stuff that dreams are made of," intones Humphrey Bogart at the end of *The Maltese Falcon*. His own line? Not a word of it: it's a quote from Shakespeare. Who doesn't know at least one of the plays of Shakespeare, or hasn't heard a phrase — a book title or a snatch from a film — originating from one of those plays? Not just the arts, but our whole language and culture are riddled with the influence of this one sixteenth-century English playwright.

Similarly, America bears the imprint of Thomas Jefferson's intellect in her *Declaration of Independence*, and the whole world bears the consequences of the scientific discoveries we associate with the names of Rutherford and Einstein. Instances proliferate. The works of Plato. Countless Ph.D. theses scattered throughout the world's universities. Every single book in every single library. Supremely, without doubt, the Bible.

Information survives also in far less glamorous settings. The stories you tell about your childhood and parents join a much larger body of stories, worn smooth by retelling, about your parents and your distant forebears. You become the custodian of these stories when you reach adulthood, and almost without thinking you pass them down to your own children. Every family does it, and if no one can remember the identity of such and such a person in the brown and fading photograph taken by your great-grandfather, you feel a palpable loss.

The ability to pass on — to give — information furnishes one of the cornerstones of civilization. Wisdom becomes encoded in proverbs (what, after all, is "look before you leap" but the benefit of somebody else's experience?). Long distant generations passed on skill within families and trades — stonemasonry, musketry, wheel-making. The fact that we now pass on equivalent skills — architecture, marksmanship, advanced rocket science — in schools and colleges, and refer to them as disciplines, indicates a shift only in the channels by which the information moves, not a diminishment of its role. Indeed, information has become so extensive, so complex, that any single individual can master only a small portion of it. Nevertheless, information as a whole represents an indispensable resource.

2. Make friendship your road

World Christian statesman, Dr. Han Kyung Chik, astonishes people who meet him because of his unassuming behavior. He stays in the mountains of Korea with his daughter and son-in-law, doing his work, his study, and his sleeping all in a single room no larger than a normal size living room in the United States.

But this man's influence is felt around the world. His church regards him so highly that they built him a posh residence on the Young Nak Presbyterian Church property. In that area, at current prices, the residence would command a million-dollar value — or more. He declined to live there. He understands and lives out the truth that "a man's life consisteth not in the abundance of things which he possesseth." Dr. Han has raised millions-dollars for the Lord's work around the world. He has built colleges, orphanages, middle schools, homes for the disadvantaged; not a dollar has stuck to his hands.

In 1975, the North Koreans and South Koreans met at Pyongyang to discuss the establishment of a cross-border mail service. The very first question the North Korean delegation asked — and the delegation included some who had been party to the persecution of Dr. Han — was "How is the Reverend Han Kyung Chik?"

When the floods ripped through Johnstown, Pennsylvania, in July, 1977, killing 68 people, the first help for the flood victims came from the Young Nak Presbyterian Church, Dr. Han's church in Seoul, Korea. Begun with 27 refugees, that church today has 60,000 members. Why did they wish to help the flood victims of Pennsylvania? Because the people of Pennsylvania had shown kindness to Dr. Han when he was a student in the United States.

Like information, relationships make up a powerful resource. In many cases relationships become themselves the channels through which information moves.   But relationships do far more than transfer information; they also establish trust, credibility, influence, power to focus many people's energies on a single purpose.   Isn't professional politics about building a base of relationships?   Ask any successful individual the secret of his success, and he will almost certainly name, not a book or a philosophy, but a person, a relationship.

The problem a corporate leader faces in securing the company ethos for future generations, and the problem every parent faces in transferring values intact to his or her children, turn out, on closer examination, to be one and the same.   They both involve developing and investing in the resource of relationship.

Paul Meyer has designed his management structure to accomplish the task at hand.   More than that, he has designed it to ensure that all the top executives in the company are enabled to operate at full potential — even when Paul Meyer can no longer give them advice.   We have a name for the process: replication — empowering others to do what you have done, teaching others to do what you do superbly, performing as you perform, with the same or even greater quantity, quality, and attitude.

"I have a president in charge of each of my companies," says Paul.   "They give me a president's report once a month.   It's never more than about two pages.   They tell me the 'state of the union,' and if there is a problem, I tell them 'Don't ask me the solution, because I know the solution.   The trick is: do you know the solution?'   I want to teach them."

Significantly, Paul estimates that a quarter of his friends are teenagers and people under twenty-five.   That's unusual for a man in his sixties.   But he deliberately spends time in ministries for youth: the Success Club, the Achievement Club, PTS, the Boys and Girls Club, the Boy Scouts. and the LaRue Learning Center.   He intends not just to "stay young," but to bridge the generation gap with real, substantive relationships.

He recalls a lesson taught him by a wealthy European friend. Paul took the man aside at a Pier 66 charitable reception and said, "I want to ask you something, Sean.   Why do you bother with all this? You've got more money than all these people put together.   Why

*Paul talking to children from the LaRue Learning Center, and joining
the kids at another charity he supports, the Waco Community Center.
He estimates that a quarter of his friends are teenagers and people under
twenty-five.*

don't you go and live happily ever after on one of your Greek
islands?" Paul was being deliberately provocative, and he received
a provocative answer. Sean replied, "When I was five years old, my
old dad took me to the poor section of town and told me, 'But for the
grace of God you and I would be living here. Never forget that God
wants us to use our lives helping these people and everyone else
who needs ministering to.' That made a profound impact on my
life."

The message moves on.   "In turn, that made an indelible impression on me," says Paul.   "And it's what I'm doing with my family now.   Every time we minister to somebody I have one of my children or one of my grandchildren there.   Like this family I helped last week.   I called my daughter Janna and asked her to come.   I wanted her to be there so she could see her father and mother ministering to somebody one-on-one, not just writing checks."

The last time Paul went to East Waco he took his son Billy's children, Adam and Christie, and joined a group of Christian young people singing and acting on the street.   "I wanted my grandchildren to see me in some role besides chairman of the board.   So they saw me over there with black youngsters and Hispanic youngsters, acting like a duck and quacking and singing children's Christian songs.   They were laughing their heads off, but what I was doing was ministering to them.   When we got in the car again I told them that everything we have is God's, and He's using us as His instruments.   And everything you study, you're studying to be His disciple.   My point is, I wouldn't have done that if it weren't for what Sean told me at Pier 66."

Too many of us seriously underestimate the need for this kind of investment in other people.   Permanence does not reside in structures and constitutions, because structures and constitutions can be changed.   Examine our major seats of learning — the Harvards and Princetons: revered as they are, you'll find little to remind you of the ideals of the men who first founded and endowed them.   Significantly, those institutions whose spirit has remained constant through the generations — Moody Bible Institute is a good example — have seen few changes of leadership and have prepared each new leader with consummate care.

Recently Paul Meyer made another key move in planning for the future of his charitable work.   Knowing the importance of unofficial leadership in the Boys and Girls Clubs, and knowing also that he wouldn't always be around to provide it, he asked his son Larry to help out.   "I know you're busy," he said.   "I know you're climbing Mt. Everest, on a fast track.   But your dad needs you now."   Since that day, Larry hasn't missed a single meeting.   As Paul intended, the challenge brought Larry further into the loop of giving.

Paul wants to pass on the gift of giving not just for the sake of

Paul celebrates his 65th birthday with his family. He intends to pass on the gift of giving.

the charities, but for others who have yet to discover the joy of open-hearted generosity. "I would like to be a role model to my family, my associates, and other business people, to run their lives in a Christlike fashion and their businesses with Christian principles. It is my hope they would dedicate a far greater part of their earnings to stewardship, both from their companies and individually."

You will allow me a preacher's leeway if I point out that Jesus Christ — who arguably has altered the course of history more profoundly than any other individual — left the world at His death with neither funds nor a definitive text. He left only twelve men. Relationships.

3. Don't leave it all behind

That said, this book seeks to highlight the giving not of information or influence, but of money, and it is to the bequeathing of financial resources that I now want to turn.

Andrew Carnegie more than once expressed the view that wealth should be given away in life, not in death. He doesn't pull his punches:

It may fairly be said that no man is to be extolled for doing what he cannot help doing, nor is he to be thanked by the community to which he only leaves wealth at death. Men who leave vast sums in this way may fairly be thought men who would not have left it at all, had they been able to take it with them.[35]

Carnegie himself gave away 90 percent of his fortune before he died. Paul intends to leave this world with nothing more to his name than he can fit in a suitcase. Both, however, have taken steps to ensure that the wealth they have generated remains protected and available for charitable use.

Protecting money is serious business. "Multiple divorces, alimony, precious gift giving, law suits, riotous parties, resplendent mansions, and parasitic entourages," notes Frederic Cople Jaher, "eroded the patrimonies of Horace Dodge, Jr., Evelyn Walsh McLean, Atwater Kent, and John Jacob Astor VI." However, he goes on, "these individual cases of pecuniary self-destruction are overshadowed by the Vanderbilt record."[36]

Cornelius Vanderbilt in 1877 and his son in 1885 left what were then the largest legacies ever recorded in America. But these resources were systematically squandered, and by the fourth and fifth generation, in the 1920s, no Vanderbilts were among the ten wealthiest Americans. In 1923, only three appeared among the 274 U.S. taxpayers with incomes in excess of a million dollars. In the 1930s, fifth-generation Cornelius Vanderbilt, Jr., predicted glumly that "In another ten years there won't be a single great fortune left in America."[37] He was mistaken. But it's food for thought that "had Vanderbilt's original $100 million in 1877 been kept intact and reinvested in the leading growth sectors of the American economy, its size a century later would be simply beyond reckoning."[38]

By contrast, Andrew Carnegie, who liquidated his $250 million business interests in 1901 to devote himself to selecting and supervising objects of philanthropy, soon found his annual income of $12.5 million too large an amount to administer in the time available. It was Carnegie, therefore, who pioneered the solution of creating a series of perpetual trusts for the support of education, scientific research, international peace, and various other causes.

Rockefeller followed suit. Like Carnegie, he detested high society extravagance, but unlike Carnegie he had made a habit of giving as early as the 1850s when he first brought home a wage. He gave away over half his fortune before he died — a fortune whose value peaked at around a billion dollars in 1913. In addition to that, he established a series of foundations and institutes between 1900 and 1914 to oversee the long-term distribution of his charitable funds. It underlines the importance of relationships. This stands in pointed contrast to the Vanderbilts; giving in the Rockefeller family has become dynastic. "I have been brought up to believe," said John D. Rockefeller, Jr., "that giving ought to be entered into in just the same careful way as investing — that giving is investing, and that it should be tested by the same intelligent standard."

After Rockefeller came numerous others: William Randolph Hearst, Sr., Alfred I. duPont, Charles Hayden, Marshall Field III, James B. Duke, Payne Whitney, Julius Rosenwald, Alfred Sloan, George Eastman, James A. Chapman, Clint Mellon, Henry Ford, William P. Moody. Before 1910, the foundations with a minimum of $100,000 in assets numbered only 36. Another 288 appeared during the 1930s, often used as tax shelters and to retain control of corporate stock. By 1962, there were 14,685, and by 1976, 26,000 — 2,818 of them with assets topping a million dollars.

The charitable institute/foundation is here to stay. But if you think of such things as the preserve of the ultrarich, think again. Almost anyone can found one — and probably many of us should.

4. Take on a trust

"The growing disposition to tax more and more heavily large estates left at death is a cheering indication of the growth of a salutary change in public opinion," Andrew Carnegie once wrote.[39]

He goes on to describe then-current British proposals to introduce increased and graduated death-duties:

> Of all forms of taxation, this seems the wisest. Men who continue hoarding great sums all their lives, the proper use of which for public ends would work good to the community, should be made to feel that the community, in the form of the state, cannot thus be deprived of its proper share. By taxing estates heavily at death the state marks its condemnation of the selfish millionaire's unworthy life.

> This policy would work powerfully to induce the rich man
> to attend to the administration of wealth during his life, which
> is the end that society should always have in view, as being
> that by far most fruitful for the people.[40]

One wonders how quickly today's wealthy Americans would applaud him.   Brought up in a poor working-class district in Dunfermline, Scotland, Carnegie disliked ostentatious wealth.   In his view, those blessed with financial resources owed a natural debt to society — a debt which the state was entitled to call in.

Whether one should draw as close an equation as Carnegie did between society and the state is another question.   Many would take issue with the assumption that death duties paid to the Treasury Department comprise, in fact, contributions to the common good. For one thing, government spends money on all kinds of projects, some of which, it could be argued, bring little benefit to the man or woman in the street.   For another, a suspicion prevails today that the priorities and ideals of the state's social arm differ markedly from those of the taxpayer.

Not surprisingly, perhaps, one of the main attractions of founding charitable trusts today lies in their power to reduce overall tax liability.   Carnegie's psychology is sound: fear of tax does indeed "induce the rich man to attend to the administration of wealth during his life."   Death will snatch it from you anyway; why not have the pleasure of giving it away yourself before you go?

Here some will point out that the desire to avoid tax hardly seems a worthy motive for philanthropy.   Paul Meyer will tell you that tax advantages play absolutely no part in his decision to give — that he simply never thinks about them.   "I wouldn't belittle my philanthropy by doing that.   I think that would be an insult to God, because I wouldn't be giving for the right reason.   I'd give the same amount if I didn't get a tax deduction."

This selflessness, to many of the insiders, at least, sets Paul Meyer apart as an extraordinarily impressive philanthropist.   It marks him as a man of principle.   Yet, as we saw earlier, we should not mistakenly insist that deriving personal benefit from giving is intrinsically wrong, or that it somehow devalues the gift.   Paul may care nothing for his tax-deductible status, but he still derives enormous benefit from his philanthropy simply because he finds it pleasurable.

"The joy of giving is better than anything I've ever done," he says. So much so that "I feel selfish every time somebody comes here and Jane and I help them."

There exist a number of financial instruments available for making deductible charitable contributions. Some of these, like charitable gift annuities, are offered by nonprofit organizations (a children's hospital, for instance) which function in this particular respect as a savings institution. Typically you sign over a capital sum (which being directed to charitable purposes offers you substantial tax deductions) in exchange for a preset and partially tax-deductible annuity.

Comparable tax advantages, however, as well as permanence of contribution beyond your own death, can be achieved by setting up your own private foundation. You can find further details of this in Appendix 3. But basically a private foundation is a separate legal entity (a trust or a nonprofit corporation) formed and controlled by a person or a family, and qualified to support a wide range of charitable work in accordance with the donor's wishes. Though it differs from a public charity (it does not have to raise public funds), it qualifies for the same tax-exempt status under the Internal Revenue Code, and any donations made to it are deductible as charitable contributions for federal income tax purposes.

Once you have decided what returns you want to achieve, setting up a private foundation presents few difficulties. A wide range of purposes will support an exemption under Section 501(c)(3) of the Internal Revenue Code. The conduct of the foundation remains subject only to a number of legal restrictions, or "operational limitations," chief among which is self-dealing. The governing document sets the limitations on the foundation's execution of the grantor's will. It also includes clear and explicit parameters regarding the provisions for the family or the named trustee(s) who administer the foundation's resources after the donor's death.

If you wish, you can even give it your own name.

12

THE GIVER WHO MAKES NO EXCUSES

Paul Meyer has never made excuses. He makes no excuses over giving. And yet if you ask the average person to give you're more likely to get an excuse than money. Here, then, are four short affirmations you'll need to overcome the most common hang-ups people have with giving.

1. "I *do* have the potential to generate a big income"

That's right. You have more potential than you think.

Meet Theodore Johnson. At the age of 90, Johnson donated half of his $70-million fortune to education. Much of the money will go to students from middle-class backgrounds who fail to qualify for government aid and whose families can't afford to support them. He has targeted it to the deaf, the disadvantaged, and American Indian students. A sizeable proportion — $7.2 million — will be distributed through the employees of the United Parcel Service — an organization Johnson worked for until he retired in 1972.[41]

A multimillionaire employee? You'd better believe it. Johnson's finishing salary, as UPS vice president for industrial relations, barely topped $14,000. He made his fortune not as a manager, but as an investor. During his working life he bought as much UPS stock as he could afford, and when the company expanded after his retirement, he watched the value of his holdings soar.

Potential, then, can remain hidden. In fact, the whole idea of potential is slightly misleading. Ask Paul Meyer where he acquired his knack for sales showmanship, and he will tell you he learned it.

"My first vision of showmanship was seeing my father on the stage as a magician in a lodge in Michigan. Also seeing him display and explain a key machine he was selling, or something he had made. He seemed like he turned into a different person. He had such a great flair."

Paul, age 19, with his mother, Isabelle Rutherford Meyer. She remains among the most powerful influences on his thinking.

A few years later, as a sales executive, Paul consciously cultivated his father's techniques. "I feel that everyone is packaged differently," says Paul," and that we all have some magic or something special and unique. Many people could have a more colorful, exciting, dramatic, and enthusiastic life, in both work and play, if they would let their child out, so to speak, and break their inhibitions, and not be so shackled to the norms of what other people say, think, or do."

Another characteristic of potentials, of course, is that they can be turned to good or ill. "You're going to end up in one of two ways," a school coach once told Paul Meyer, "either highly successful, or in the penitentiary."

By this time the young Meyer had already instituted a goals program for excelling in basketball. Unable to afford a hoop for his back yard, he persuaded a cousin who'd taken a welding course to construct a hoop for him. So he could practice after dark, Paul also attached a light to a nearby tree. He shot baskets by the hour.

"Man, you are an attacker," the coach once said. "You just ran right over that guy to score."

Paul went home angry and said to his mother, "Let me tell you what Coach Hill said."

His mother listened, then replied, "I think Coach Hill is right."

"Why do you say that?"

"Because you have such a strong personality. Look in the mirror. Look in your eyes." She said, "You are not going to see many eyes that can be as intense as yours. It's a gift. You can either use it for good or use it for evil."

Paul used it for good. When he switched from weekly premium to ordinary insurance, he set himself a goal to sell a million in the first year. He tracked his progress using 3x5 cards, adding a plus or minus sign each month to tell him whether he was ahead of or behind schedule. He ended the year with $165,000 sold ahead of his goal. The next year, in which he'd planned to double his sales, he sold $3,800,000 — so much that he had to keep adjusting the goal upward as the year progressed.

He sees this determination now as slightly obsessive. But his example points out that even Paul's success owes much to hard work and organization. You may not make $70 million by your ninetieth birthday, like Theodore Johnson; but you have the potential to bring in a lot more than you're making now.

2. "It *is* worth giving small amounts"

I've mentioned a good many big-name philanthropists in this book. "But," you may say, "these people you mention are worth millions. I'd give, too, if I had millions." Let me tell you: most of them started off with nothing, and they started giving long before they were wealthy. John D. Rockefeller, for instance, tithed while he was an assistant bookkeeper earning the vast sum of $50.00 for three months' work. Don't wait to start giving.

One Sunday afternoon in the 1880s, a six-year-old girl by the name of Hattie Wiatt got turned away from the Sunday school at Grace Baptist Church on Philadelphia's Berks and Mervine. The church occupied a small site, many families attended, and the Sunday school classes were full. Bitterly disappointed, Hattie resolved that, if she could not attend the existing Sunday school, she would save her pennies and build a new one.

She picked out a small red purse, and every week put into it a large portion of her pocket money. Not long afterwards she became seriously ill. But before she died she told her mother about the purse, and made her promise to give the money to Grace Baptist Church on condition that it be used for the purpose she intended. The purse contained just 57 cents.

The next Sunday the minister, Dr. Russell Conwell, relayed this information to a silent congregation.

"When we heard how God had blessed us with so great an inheritance," said a member of the congregation later, "there was silence — the silence of tears and earnest consecration. We felt that the cornerstone of a new church was laid."

Hattie Wiatt's tiny legacy precipitated the church's decision to build not just a new Sunday school, but a whole new complex. This was no light task. The congregation consisted mostly of working men and women who could not afford to make large donations to a building fund. But Hattie Wiatt's example inspired them to save. Tired men, muscles aching from a hard day's work, and women weary from a long day spent at a typewriter or a shop counter, cheerfully trudged home on foot to save the nickels. They gave up smoking and gave their tobacco money. They stayed home over summer and gave their vacation money. Innumerable entertainments were held. A fair was put on in one of the largest halls of Philadelphia, in the central part of the city, attracting thousands of visitors and netting nearly $9,000.

Finally in September 1886, they purchased the lot at Broad and Berks for $25,000. The ground was broken on March 27, 1889, the cornerstone laid on July 13, 1890. On that site in a few years stood the Baptist Temple of Philadelphia. "During the opening exercises, over nine thousand people were present at each service," said the Philadelphia Press, describing the opening. "The very air seemed to thrill with thanksgiving that day." As well it should. The down payment on the site? Just 57 cents.

The poignancy of the story, of course, rests on the courage of a small child. For that reason it has a slightly magical, fairy-tale feel about it. But the principle it embodies — of the exemplary power of giving — stands true for adults as much as for children. It also shows clearly how an apparently impossible goal can be achieved on the strength of small donations. Ask the fund-raisers: you won't find one of them who despises a $5 gift. In many cases $5 gifts support a million- dollar project.

If you think it's "not worth giving small amounts," the chances are you're making an excuse of your low income, and need to work on a third affirmation.

3. "I *can* afford to give now"

Most of our unwillingness to give finds its source in this sentiment. We already feel stretched. We already go without things we'd like to have. We already feel guilty at asking our families to tighten their belts. Why complicate things by giving money away?

Bear in mind three facts.

One, it's better to give a little than to give nothing at all. And I mean better for you as well as for others. You may start by setting aside what looks to you an impossibly small amount. But merely by setting it aside you gain a sense of control over your finances. You begin to grasp the discipline.

Two, there are few people so poor that they can't give at least a little. Businessman Frank Madia began giving in his late teens, when he received just $55 a week in the form of an unemployment check. He gave a tithe of 10 percent. Today, at age forty, Frank has gone into property development and has raised the percentage to between 25 percent and 30 percent. He sees the discipline of giving, and his financial success, as intimately connected.

Three, it's a blatant reversal of the truth to say that giving keeps you poor. Givers prosper. If you commit yourself to the discipline of giving you will end up receiving more than you've given out. Remember, giving isn't expenditure; it's investment.

Chuck Williams, president of one of the Meyer family companies, has made a study of personal finance. As he sees it, most people have gotten into the habit of burdening themselves with debt repayment. They borrow, and as a result the money they could have given or saved gets paid to their creditors as interest.

"It has very little to do with your income level; it has more to do with your spending patterns. The concept we have had in America for a number of years now is that it doesn't matter if you spend 105 percent of what you make, because next year you're going to get a 10 percent raise, and it will take care of itself. The problem is that next year you spend 105 percent again, and it goes up and up."

In 1945, an executive from one of the major oil companies drove me back to Chicago, Illinois, after I had preached in a little city named Pekin, about 175 miles away.

"Young preacher," He said, "you did all right tonight. In fact, I found your sermon interesting. I think you have a bright future. Live out your faith. Honor the Lord. Work hard. You'll do well." Then he added, "Just one caution. Don't ever mention money. Talking about money will kill a church dead as a dodo. Take me, for instance. I used to tithe my income, but now my income is so large I can't afford to tithe."

I've recounted the following to many friends over the years. I said, "Stop the car!"

He pulled over, stunned.

I told him, "Now let's pray that God will cut back your income to where you can once again afford to tithe."

He couldn't escape the incontrovertible logic of the implication. Tithing comes down to discipline whether you rub shoulders with the superrich or bring home a hard-earned weekly paycheck from the steelworks. If a poor person can give, no one well endowed with financial resources can pretend giving is impossible. In fact, even in terms of percentage, the wealthy can give far more.

Paul Meyer's first lessons on stewardship came from his mother, and later from his friend Lee Boswell. He'd begun tithing after he heard his first pastor, at Wayside Baptist Church in Florida, preach on the subject. Sometime later, he heard an address by famed industrialist R.G. LeTourneau. Paul couldn't believe what the man was saying. LeTourneau gave 90 percent of his income.

Paul recalls his reaction. "I thought I was right on the verge of being a generous person because I was giving twenty percent. And this man said he was giving 90 percent. I thought, 'If I had ten percent left, I would be living in a tent.'"

But LeTourneau's testimony inspired Paul to increase giving percentage into a life goal. He made the decision just weeks before his partner Basil Autrey disappeared and Paul plunged himself into debt to sort out the financial debacle at National Union. Yet, in the longer term, his commitment to giving got him out of the hole.

"I never lost my belief, trust, or faith, and I've never missed a

,pledge from that day to this, regardless of other circumstances. I simply put pledges first. Giving does something for me that nothing else could do. In a lifetime I would simply say the more I have poured out, the more I have had to pour out; and the more I give, the more I have to give. And I am not just talking about blessing in the form of financial return."

Every year since he left National Union, Paul Meyer has given a higher percentage. He constantly finds new role models. Bernard Rapoport, a neighbor and friend, has taught him much about establishing foundations. Recently he has enjoyed the influence of another colleague, Paul Piper. Paul Meyer knows givers don't go short.

Regrettably, few have followed his example. A survey taken in the United States in the late 1970s revealed that doctors give a lower percentage of their income than any other group. Second worst on the list? Preachers! I know many generous doctors, and I know many generous preachers. But for fifteen years I've pondered why so many in these two categories give so little. I have concluded it's because they think they already give so much after-hours' time and free assistance. They cop out of giving money, and in so doing fall prey to self-delusion and deprive themselves of life-transforming enrichment. The question isn't whether they can afford to give. It's whether they can afford not to.

4. "Giving *isn't* for suckers"

Paul was putting gas in his airplane one day when a boy came up and said, "I've been wanting to thank you."

Not recognizing him, Paul said, "For what?"

"I did a favor for you four years ago. I didn't tell you then, but I'd just quit school. You gave me a hundred bucks and thanked me for taking care of your airplane. I used that money to buy some school books that same afternoon. I felt God was telling me to go back to school. I graduated, and now I have a job with a petroleum company. And it would have never happened if it were not for that hundred dollars."

On another occasion, Paul recalls, "I got a call from a girl at North Texas State College. She said to my assistant, 'Tell Mr. Meyer thank you. I have just graduated from college. Most of all thank him for changing my looks.' So my assistant said, 'What do you mean?' And then the girl said, 'He paid for getting my teeth capped.'"

Suddenly Paul bursts out laughing.

"Now I'm telling you, sitting here today, I do not remember that situation at all. But that has happened to me five hundred times. And they'll come up later and thank me, and I don't know who they are."

"Paul seems to take it for granted," comments Paul Meyer's biographer Gladys Hudson, "that seeing a need defines his opportunity to help. From my observation, I can tell you that Paul is thoroughly sincere in expressing this attitude. His stewardship is never tinged with the desire to manipulate or coerce other people. He trusts people and cares for them sometimes almost to the point of naivete."

Which is surely problematic. The more generous you are, after all, the more easily you will be taken for a ride. Isn't generous just another word for "sucker"? The question arose during an executive training session at Paul's country property, Summers Mill. Somebody asked Jane Meyer if anyone took advantage of her husband, and how she felt about it.

Jane, a clever and attractive woman, feels strongly. "It does happen," she replied. "He always tells me that it doesn't really matter and that the important thing is for him to be doing things for people. But I said that it's taking advantage of him. I don't think it's fair, and, yes, I get mad about it."

Paul himself is laid back. He recalls an example. An employee told him her husband just had a heart attack. What should she do? Without blinking, Paul replied "Go home and take care of your husband. He may die." He arranged to pay her full salary for six months. The husband died almost immediately, and the woman came back and quit the next week. Nevertheless Paul kept his word.

Some people criticized him. "Don't you feel like a fool, Meyer, that you paid this woman?"

He replied, "No, I feel wonderful. In fact, I feel better about helping her than anybody I've helped before. My goodness, do you think I paid her so she'd feel she owed me something? She doesn't owe me a dime. I'll get paid back in this world, or my children's world, or by laying up treasure for myself in Heaven."

He still feels that way.   "Everybody joked about it in the company, what a dumb-ox I was because I helped her, and that she quit the next day. But I felt good about it. The point is, I would have helped her even if she didn't work for me. It made no difference."

Scripture backs him up. Paul Meyer often quotes 1 Timothy 6:17-19: "Command those who are rich in this present age . . . to do good, to be rich in good works, ready to give, willing to share, storing up for themselves a good foundation for the time to come, that they may lay hold on eternal life."

As the Minnesota banker George M. Palmer once observed, "I know that I very often get taken in by someone who is unworthy. But I would rather be an easy mark than a meat-axe."

EPILOGUE

WHAT WILL HISTORY SAY ABOUT YOU IN THE YEAR 2099?

L ook back through the ages and you'll find that history has numerous ways of cutting humanity in half. The introverts and the extroverts. The rich and the poor. The hairy and the bald. But perhaps the most persistent and far-reaching distinction is the one between the givers and the takers.

I have on the desk in front of me a book of speeches by a man named Keir Hardie. Like Paul Meyer, Hardie was a self-made man, and came from the same stock. Born to a Scottish mining family in the mid-nineteenth century, Hardie started working in the pits while still a boy, and taught himself to read and write by scratching letters on smoke-blackened slate. He became a politician — the first to enter the British House of Commons clad in a working-man's cap rather than the obligatory top hat. Long before that, however, the upper classes had learned to fear his keen sense of justice and his acid wit.

When the Duke of Hamilton died in May, 1895, Hardie wrote an obituary.[42] Dukes in general did not attract Hardie's compassion. This one turned his stomach.

Hardie began the obituary by listing — exhaustively — all the titles by which the deceased Duke had liked to be addressed.

"The Right Hon. Sir William Alexander Louis Stephen Douglas-Hamilton, twelfth Duke of Hamilton and ninth Duke of Brandon, Marquis of Douglas and Clydesdale, Earl of Angus, Arran, Lanark, and. . ." (I will spare you the rest of the places the Duke ruled over) "Baron of Dutton in the county of Chester, Duke of Chatelherault, Hereditary Keeper of Holyrood House, Premier Peer, and Knight Marischal of Scotland. This onerously betitled man," Hardie informed his readers, "is dead."

Why exactly did this self-regarding Duke need an obituary?

"He came," wrote Hardie, "from a long line of ancestors whose historic record proves that they were vacillating, shifty and treacherous when it served their purpose. Failing the Stuart line, he was next in succession to the crown of Scotland. It is not easy, however, to discover in any of these things any claim to our gratitude. Nor did his enormous wealth add to his worth as a citizen."

The opposite. In retrospect, Hardie found it extraordinary that the Duke's workers should have submitted to ". . . a rule under which this dead man was able, not only to extract hundreds of thousands a year from the wealth produced by their labor, but to say that they should not be able to labor at all without his permission."

I am not concerned here with Hardie's political views.[43] For my present purposes, they are immaterial. Nor does it matter whether he represented the deceased Duke fairly (though no doubt the Duke's friends found plenty with which to take issue). My point is simply this: a hundred years or so after the event, the picture we receive of the Duke of Hamilton looks irredeemably black. He was a scoundrel. History — in the person of Keir Hardie — has passed its judgment on him, and he stands roundly condemned. He "extracted hundreds of thousands a year." He was a taker, of the worst sort.

Gazing back over the millennia, the same could be said of too many prominent figures. Whatever their flatterers may have told them at the time, the fact that we append to their names words like "despot" and "tyrant" indicates that, as history sees them, they concerned themselves with taking, with what they could get. They seized power. They diverted national wealth to their private use. They separated their citizens from liberty and freedom, sometimes from life itself.

Josef Stalin marks only the far point of a very long scale punctuated by (among others) dictators, drunken husbands, extremist religious leaders, and petty bureaucratic potentates. True, one writer has asked us recently to admire Attila the Hun as a paradigm of incisive leadership. But the writer has his tongue poked firmly into his cheek. Dear old Attila only made it into the annals of modern management by trading on his reputation as a merciless cutthroat.

By the same token, set against the likes of Attila, we have another group of people whom history festoons with a rosy aura of saintliness. The roll call traditionally begins with Mother Teresa of Calcutta and winds its way through such innocents and moral luminaries as Florence Nightingale, David Livingstone, Albert

Einstein, Mahatma Gandhi, Francis of Assisi, even Beatrix Potter.

We do not easily think of such individuals as prey even to small vices. They belong to that noble company called "the great and the good," and were we ever asked to justify the existence of the human race, theirs are the names which would immediately spring to our lips.

What distinguishes them, of course, and binds them together, is their giving. Look at the language we use to describe them. We speak of Einstein *giving* the world the General Theory of Relativity (never mind what else he wrapped up in the gift). Florence Nightingale *gave* herself to the service of the wounded at Crimea. Beatrix Potter *gave* us Jemima Puddleduck and Peter Rabbit.

We put these names up in lights. And of course there are countless more. Most of us can think of at least one other person we love because he or she has given us so much. Why else do many of us fondly remember our parents? As soon as we have children ourselves we realize what an unstinting act of self-sacrifice parenthood can be. To use Keir Hardie's words, we understand that those who are committed to giving possess "a claim to our gratitude."

Giving doesn't only win you the approval of others. It also makes you happy. Paul Meyer, the supreme giver, the millionaire who plans to die with nothing left to give, is an irrepressibly happy man.

"I am happy when I am completing a fifty-mile bike ride. I am happy when I am flying my airplane. I am happy when I am scuba diving. I am happy when I see all my friends have a good time. I am happy when I know that my pastor, our youth minister, and young people from our church go to the West Retreat to spend the night. I am happy when I hear stories — in the form of letters, phone calls, and from the platform — that people's lives have been changed from using our programs. I am happy when I see people developing their full potential and growing as executives in our company, and learning to be better communicators and successful executives. I am happy that I have been instrumental in helping so many women climb the corporate ladder and reach dreams that very few would think possible in their careers. I guess I would expand the word 'happy' to joy, excitement, thrill, and fulfillment."

Paul Meyer's giving is open and honest. It cannot be confused with the phenomenon I call "yo-yo giving" — financial commitment

Paul relaxing with friends. Bike riding and business make him equally happy.

Paul celebrates the thousandth landing of his Piper Cub.

made with a great song and dance and then quietly reneged upon.

Let me give you an example of yo-yo giving. A couple pledged a million dollars to a university in Texas. The news media gave them front-page attention because of the size of the gift. This was more than 30 years ago when a million dollars amounted to $4.6 million in today's dollars. The donors paid the first $100,000 installment. They never paid another dime. Nor did they intend to when they made the commitment. Where could they have acquired the kind of benefit for $100,000 that they gained in pledging the one million dollars?   First of all, it gave them credibility among the financial institutions who thought they must have enormous resources.   Second, it gave them the attention of business and civic groups, who put on testimonial dinners for them and gave them prestigious awards. Third, it catapulted them to the top echelon of the social elite in their city.

To say that the couple did actually give $100,000, and that this was after all no mean sum, barely excuses what from any angle was a piece of cynical advantage-taking.   But do vanity, guilt, or cool manipulation invalidate a gift?   The answer is no — unless, of course, the beneficiary in the end receives nothing and the gift turns out not to have been a gift after all.   Mixed motives, however, can do something else: they can narrow the donor's vision to the immediate and the obvious.   The yo-yo givers had no real desire to advance the cause of education.   True, their check didn't bounce.   But by looking for "front-end" benefits — by being myopic — the yo-yo givers failed to realize the full potential of giving, both for themselves and for others.

I suggest to you that once history has closed on the twentieth century the couple who gave that $100,000 will be remembered not as givers, but as takers.   In lying, in breaking trust, they took from society infinitely more than they gave in dollars and cents.   They mark the opposite end of the scale from Paul Meyer.

And that, perhaps, is the crucial distinction.   Between the person who gives occasionally, as a calculated strategy or when he or she has money to spare, and the person who has so internalized giving that it becomes integral to his or her entire lifestyle, including financial planning.   The one thinks in terms of the risks of giving; the other knows that giving ultimately guarantees success.   The one is afraid to give; the other is reassured that giving is "safe."   One is a person who gives.   The other is a giver.

Gladys Hudson, Paul Meyer's biographer and a top executive in the Meyer family companies, knows what it means to have the spirit of giving.

"Paul Meyer told me one day this week that he had discovered an important truth.   He said that when he takes care of people with whom he associates, there is no need to give thought to a return on his investment of time, money, or effort.   He said this has freed him to act from love and caring for other people. He finds it easier to be creative in discovering ways to provide opportunities and support for the people around him. The result is, he told me, that his needs are cared for as well. When he provides generous compensation to people who work for him, takes an interest in their personal needs and supports and helps them, the natural result is that they are productive in their jobs; as a result, his business prospers. I can tell you from my own experience with Paul that this is true."

So ask yourself the "history question." Were somebody to read about you in a hundred years' time, as we read about the Duke of Hamilton through the journalism of Keir Hardie, what impression would he or she form? Which of that conflicting tangle of motives in your heart will be most visible to generations to come? Will you be a David, or a Saul? A Mary, or a Delilah? On balance, will you look like a giver, or a taker?

I know how Paul Meyer will be remembered. I have absolutely no doubt that future generations will garland his life with praise. For he is by heart and soul a giver.

He said to me recently, "When I get to the age of 70 or 80 or 90, I want to be able to say that I amounted to something, that I made a difference in the world. I want to be the best I can be for God. I want to fan the flame of love for God among my family, my friends, and my associates. Jane's and my message to our children is 'Join us in serving, for Christ's sake, for God's purpose.' I want to be known by my children and grandchildren, even a hundred years from now, as a man who walked with God and lived for Christ. I want to be a minister for the Lord, a servant for Jesus Christ. I want to do the unusual for God, knowing that He will do the incredible for me. . . ."

What do *you* want? Think long and hard.

APPENDICES

APPENDIX 1: Charts

FINANCIAL RETURN:	BENEFITS TO ME:	BENEFITS TO OTHERS:
RANK ( )		
RANK ( )		
RANK ( )		
RANK ( )		
RANK ( )		
RANK ( )		
RANK ( )		
RANK ( )		
RANK ( )		
RANK ( )		

Chart 1: Financial returns

INTELLECTUAL RETURN:	BENEFITS TO ME:	BENEFITS TO OTHERS:
RANK ( )		
RANK ( )		
RANK ( )		
RANK ( )		
RANK ( )		
RANK ( )		
RANK ( )		
RANK ( )		
RANK ( )		
RANK ( )		

Chart 2: Intellectual returns

RELATIONAL RETURN:	BENEFITS TO ME:	BENEFITS TO OTHERS:
RANK ( )		
RANK ( )		
RANK ( )		
RANK ( )		
RANK ( )		
RANK ( )		
RANK ( )		
RANK ( )		
RANK ( )		
RANK ( )		

Chart 3: Relational returns

PHYSICAL RETURN:	BENEFITS TO ME:	BENEFITS TO OTHERS:
RANK ( )		
RANK ( )		
RANK ( )		
RANK ( )		
RANK ( )		
RANK ( )		
RANK ( )		
RANK ( )		
RANK ( )		
RANK ( )		

Chart 4: Physical returns

SPIRITUAL RETURN:	BENEFITS TO ME:	BENEFITS TO OTHERS:
RANK ( )		
RANK ( )		
RANK ( )		
RANK ( )		
RANK ( )		
RANK ( )		
RANK ( )		
RANK ( )		
RANK ( )		
RANK ( )		

Chart 5: Spiritual returns

APPENDIX 2: Paul Meyer's letter to his daughter Leslie

Leslie,

We all run into walls, obstacles, people who think differently or have a different view or perspective. How we *act* or *react* can have *positive* or *negative* effects on our lives.

It's not what happens to us that matters, but rather, *our attitude* toward what happens.

It's imperative that we choose a proactive or positive response. Choosing forces us to gain perspective and then decide our own actions or reaction. Choosing is accepting responsibility for our own attitude and action. Choosing a *proactive response* to what people say or do is the only way to live life without blaming others or circumstance.

Unless we choose, or exercise the power to choose, our actions & behavior will be determined by conditions or what other people say, think, or do.

Leslie, real true FREEDOM is your right and your power to decide, every time, how anything or anybody outside ourselves can or will affect us.

We must always view everything from a Christian perspective (with love, compassion, concern, caring, and a forgiving attitude). This means to always distinguish between the person and the behavior or performance. We may disapprove of someone's actions or behavior, but when communicating with them it should always be to help build their self-esteem, their sense of worth, totally apart from judgments or criticism or something they said or did which we do not agree with or approve.

Leslie, when we love people — we exercise patience (1st John 4:7-8). Without loving patience, we say things we really don't mean or intend to say. Patience is expressing faith, hope, wisdom & love. Patience is trying to work things out — to smooth things over — do things together with others, in an accepting way, even though they are different, think different, have different views, and act or react differently than we would in the same situation.

Leslie, people are very tender inside, particularly those who act as if they are tough & self-sufficient — and if we will listen to them with compassion and love — listen with our heart, we can have a great influence on them. Love is attracting and magnetic. Any expression of it, *during a difference of opinion,* has a powerful influence on the other person.

And Leslie — always wish, want, and assume the very best for others. Like attracts like. When you assume other people are making every effort to do their best, *as they see it,* you can have a powerful influence and bring out the best in them. People simply tend to respond to how we treat them and more importantly, what we think & believe about them.

My mother's favorite (or one of her favorite) sayings was, "Stop and see things from the other person's point of view" or "Walk in their shoes for a while." This takes living & acting out our Christian faith with courage, patience & confidence. People will never open up or warm up to us if they feel we do not accept them for who they are — or show in any way that we do not understand them.

Leslie — if someone hurts you by something they have said or something they have done — *then you take the initiative to clear it up.*

If you don't take the initiative, things fester, expand, get blown out of proportion, people feel wounded, hurt, people brood, people act defensively to avoid more hurt. When taking the initiative, do so again with Christ's love in your heart & action (1st John 4:7-8), not in a spirit of vindictiveness or anger or a contest or to win.

And don't be afraid to describe your feelings in detail — when & how you were hurt, rather than judging the other person — always, always preserve the dignity & self-respect of the other person. Remember, no matter what we think, our feelings, opinion, and perception are not facts, in other words, showing Christian humility.

And lastly — always admit the mistake is yours, always apologize, always ask others for forgiveness, when more than one person is involved in a difference, both are partly to blame — make no excuses, no explanations, no defense. My mother always said, "Put it in the 'forgetter,'" "Throw it out the window," "Write it on paper and burn it."

Then renew your relationship — your commitment to the thing you have in common, that you enjoy participating in together, that unites you as friends. Differences aren't erased or ignored; they are put on the back shelf — the issue of proving who's right or wrong is never, never, never as important as the relationship.

Show always that you care, really care (1st John 4:7-8). Another old, old saying, Leslie, that is filled with God's wisdom, *"I don't care how much you know until I know how much you care."*

Set your mind & heart & *choose* pleasantness, good thoughts and cheerfulness. Seek to serve.

What we are, as Christians, communicates far more eloquently than what we will ever say or do.

Leslie, it's my prayer for you that you will pray and seek God's counsel, advice, & *His will* to help you solve all differences you ever have with others.

I love you.

Dad

APPENDIX 3: Three thank-you letters to Paul Meyer

From Stacy Miller. Paul Meyer woke up one morning thinking about her. Feeling she was having a tough time, he wrote to her and sent her an SMI program and a check for one thousand dollars.

Dear Meyers,

Hello, how is everyone? All is well here in Casper. I wanted to write to you and tell you what a blessing from God your family is. Yesterday I was really bummed out — worried about how to pay my car insurance and how to fix my car and how am I going to start school. Well, then I came home and got my mail!! Inspirational tapes and a one thousand dollar check! I started crying and really didn't even know how to act. The only thing I could say was "Thank you God!" over and over again. That was truly a miracle! I don't even know what to say or how to act.

I'm still going to work on going to school. The reason I'm not going already is because I'm not qualifying for a grant. The grant pays for the tuition and living expenses. That's why I'm waiting because I need to have those things for 10 1/2 months so I can be done with school. Going to school 8 to 5 everyday will take up all my time so I'd have a tuff time working and going to school. So I'm trying and the money will go to good use. No doubt about that. I also thought about helping my brother out some as he's having a tuff time finding a job and he needs to pay his car payment — it's only $112.00 so I thought I could just help him out as much as I could.

I guess I just want to say thank-you. And I don't know what else to say except that God has blessed me through you. Thank you. Love and God bless,

Stacy Miller.

A card from Maritza Crespo, Venezuela.

Dear Paul,

I have been wanting to thank you in writing for quite a while. It is funny how we don't take time to thank the people who make all the difference in the world in our lives. Five years ago you paid for my training at Haggai Institute. It was a turning point. Since then my life is divided into two periods: before and after H.I.. I was born hyper. I have always been a workaholic but, as my daughter says, now I'm both things but effectively. Now I know what I want and how to work to get it. Last October, I bought your Personal Success Planner — that I have wanted for a long time. To make a long story short, I'll be in Alabama next summer getting ready to complete my Ph.D. I might need two summers but I already have the commitment and the money to do it. I'm even becoming organized!! I will never be able to repay all you have done for me, but I want you to know there is somebody in Venezuela that loves you beyond words, that is multiplying what you invested in her, who is also praying and thanking the Lord for you and what you do every single day.

Eternally in debt,

Maritza Crespo

From Don and Pearl Anderson of Don Anderson Ministries in Tyler, Texas.

Dear Paul and Jane,

Tour is over and we have three weeks before spring tour begins. I was so glad to have you in class. I hope Jane is not having ill effects of her accident. What a miracle!

Paul, your pledge came last week and it really means a lot to us knowing that your business was down nearly half last year and yet you are faithful to the Lord in your giving and to us His servants.

I was reminded of you this morning in my devotional reading. It was in Acts 10, and Luke records about Cornelius:

10:4 "And the angel replied, "your prayers and charities have not gone unnoticed by God!"

10:2 "He was a godly man, deeply reverent, as was his entire household. He gave generously to charity and was a man of prayer."

Thanks! For your *faithful* love and friendship. We are celebrating our 20th year and you have had a significant part in all of it. May you and Jane be blessed because of it. Keep hanging in there because we are getting closer and closer to the finish line!

Joyfully,

Don & Pearl

APPENDIX 4: Setting up a private foundation

What a private foundation is.

A private foundation allows a donor to give money (and, therefore, obtain tax benefits on the amounts given) but still retain a significant amount of control over the final use of the funds. Like a public charity, a private foundation qualifies for tax exempt status under the Internal Revenue Code. Consequently, any money given to the foundation is deductible for federal income tax purposes. As what is known as a "Section 501(c)(3) organization," a private foundation can have a wide variety of purposes — charitable, educational, scientific, literary, religious. However, it cannot be a *public* charity — that is:

* A church or a convention or association of churches.
* An educational organization such as a school or university.
* A hospital or medical research organization.
* A public university development fund.
* A domestic governmental body.
* A publicly supported organization.
* An affiliate of one or more of the above.

Why set up a private foundation?

There are a number of advantages to giving through a private foundation.

(1) By transferring capital to the foundation and making suitable arrangements for future control of the fund, you ensure that your giving goes on even after you have died.
(2) You are free to specify exactly what use you want your funds put to, knowing that your choice, expressed in the foundation's governing documents, will be binding on future trustees.
(3) A private foundation allows you to make donations to individuals tax-deductible. You cannot donate a scholarship or grant directly to another individual and receive a tax deduction for the donation. But you can receive tax deductions (on awards for travel expenses or fees, for instance) if you do it through a private foundation — provided the grants are awarded in an objective and nondiscriminatory manner.

(4) Subject to certain special rules, and provided the money is used
     for charitable purposes, a private foundation can make deductible
     gifts to foreign charities and even to foreign governments.
(5) Similarly, a private foundation can gain tax deductions on gifts
     to noncharitable organizations — provided that the foundation
     exercises "expenditure responsibility" by ensuring that the
     recipient maintains the grant in a separate fund for charitable
     purposes, for instance an educational program.
(6) Subject to the "minimum payout requirement," a donor may
     accumulate contributions to a private foundation over a period
     of time in order to meet a specific high-cost charitable objective
     (for example, a university construction project).

Private foundations and tax advantage.

A private foundation acts as a financial holding-tank between
the donor and recipient. That you pay a charity through a private
foundation makes no difference to the charity: it receives the same
(usually annual) contribution you would have made if you were
paying directly. The arrangement holds definite advantages for the
donor, however. In a year when your earnings are high, producing a
correspondingly high tax liability, you can, subject to certain
"deduction limitations," put several years' contributions into the
foundation and receive the deduction for all of them in that year.

This kind of "prefunding" makes sound financial sense. The
IRS estimates that a $10,000 charitable contribution deduction by an
individual in — let's just assume — a 40 percent tax bracket cuts
taxes otherwise payable by $4,000. The same deduction by a 20
percent bracket taxpayer reduces taxes by $2,000. IRS research
indicates that "prefunding contributions may be beneficial from a
tax standpoint even if the donor's tax bracket does not drop in
future years."

How to set up a private foundation.

The first and crucial move is to decide what goal you want the
foundation to fulfil. It can be organized for any purpose that will
support an exemption under Section 501(c)(3) of the Internal Revenue
Code, and can take the form of a trust or a nonprofit corporation.
You are advised to place the legal and financial details in the hands
of qualified legal counsel and an experienced accountant.

What a private foundation may *not* do.

The foundation's governing document must state that the foundation will not expose itself to certain operational limitations. Operational limitations mark the boundaries of what the IRS holds to be good conduct in the running of a foundation. Rules prohibit any disqualified person (mainly officers of the foundation and substantial contributors) from acting in such a way as to take personal advantage of the foundation's resources or put those resources in danger.

Main offenses are the inclusion of excess business holdings, the jeopardizing of financial investments, expenditures for noncharitable purposes, and self-dealing (illicit transactions between the private foundation and disqualified persons). The IRS enforces the rules strictly through a series of excise taxes. Breaches of conduct attract an initial excise tax, ranging from 5 percent to 10 percent of the amount involved, either on the foundation or, in the case of dealing, on the disqualified person committing the offense. Those failing to correct their misconduct in a timely manner risk an additional excise tax, ranging from 25 percent to 200 percent.

In offenses other than self-dealing, the IRS has discretionary authority to abate initial excise taxes if the violation has been corrected and was due to reasonable cause and not willful neglect. According to the IRS, "experience has shown that the operational limitations do not, as a practical matter, pose a significant problem for most foundations."

APPENDIX 5: Dream planners

DREAM:
MISSION:

$	🕐	SECONDARY INVESTMENTS	PRIMARY INVESTMENTS

DREAM:
MISSION:

$	⏱	SECONDARY INVESTMENTS	PRIMARY INVESTMENTS

DREAM:
MISSION:

$	⏱	SECONDARY INVESTMENTS	PRIMARY INVESTMENTS

ENDNOTES

1   Earl V. Pierce, *The Supreme Beatitude* (New York: Fleming H. Revell, 1947) p. 18.

2   Andrew Carnegie, "Wealth," *The North American Review*, Vol. CXLVIII (June 1889) p. 656.

3   Ralph Waldo Emerson, "Compensation," in *Selected Essays* (New York: T. Nelson & Sons) p. 40.

4   Susan Watts, "Musicians created by graft, not genius," in *The Independent*, 1 September 1993.

5   Details from Edward Hungerford, *The Story of the Waldorf-Astoria* (New York and London: Putnam's Sons, 1925) pp. 28-31.

6   See John D.Watt, "The Impact of the Frequency of Ingratiation on the Performance Evaluation of Bank Personnel," in *The Journal of Psychology*, Vol. 127, No.2, 1993.

7   Aristotle, *Nicomachean Ethics* 1096a5-8.

8   Earle Pierce, *The Supreme Beatitude* (New York: Fleming H. Revell, 1947) p. 14.

9   Frederic Cople Jaher, "The Gilded Elite: American Multimillionaires, 1865 to the Present," in W.D. Rubenstein (ed), *Wealth and the Wealthy in the Modern World* (New York: St. Martin's Press, 1980) p. 194.

10 Quoted in Alasdair Clayre, *Work and Play: Ideas and Experience of Work and Leisure* (London: Weidenfeld and Nicolson, 1974) p. 191.

11 Giving, in this sense, could be regarded as a "technology." For a discussion of technology as alchemy, see Paul Zane Pilzer, *Unlimited Wealth: The Theory and Practice of Economic Alchemy* (New York: Crown Publishers, 1990).

12 Andrew Carnegie, *The Gospel of Wealth and Other Timely Essays* , ed. Edward C. Kirkland, (Cambridge, Massachusetts: The Belknap Press of Harvard University Press, 1965), p. 23.

13 Marshall Field, *Freedom is More Than a Word* (Chicago: University of Chicago Press, 1945), p. ix.

14 Carnegie, "Wealth," *North American Review*, p. 663.

15 A special note for Jim Meyer. You said, "And make sure you mention in your book that I won the Ping-Pong tournament on Leslie's birthday." There you are, Jim. Good as my word.

16 Andrew Carnegie, "The Best Fields for Philanthropy," *The North American Review*, Vol. CXLIX (December 1889) p. 691.

17 Earl V. Pierce, *The Supreme Beatitude* (New York: Fleming H. Revell, 1947) p. 65.

18 Earl V. Pierce, *The Supreme Beatitude* (New York: Fleming H. Revell, 1947) p. 28.

19 Rich Devos, *Compassionate Capitalism: People Helping People Help Themselves* (New York: Penguin Books, 1993) p. 334 (CREDO 7).

20 See "Management by Necessity" in *Inc Magazine*, March 1989, p. 33.

21 Amar Bhide and Howard H. Stevenson, "Why Be Honest if Honesty Doesn't Pay" in *Harvard Business Review*, September-October 1990, pp. 122,128.

22 Amar Bhide and Howard H.Stevenson, *op. cit.*, p. 128.

23   Amar Bhide and Howard H.Stevenson, *op. cit.*, pp. 128,129.

24   See Ivor Shapiro, "Cleaning Up" in *Saturday Night,* November 1990, p. 29.

25   See Ronni Sandroff, "How Ethical is American Business?" in *Working Woman,* September 1990, p. 114.

26   Quoted in Richard A. Rauch, "A Quality Life Should Be Full of Values" in *USA Today,* January 1990, p. 73.

27   Ivor Shapiro, *op. cit.,* p. 30.

28   See John H. Taylor, "Creative Philanthropy" in *Forbes 400,* October 19, 1992, pp. 64-66.

29   Miranda Seymour, "Generosity," in *The Independent Magazine,* 7 August 1993.

30   Norman Vincent Peale, *The True Joy of Positive Living* (New York: Morrow Publishers, 1984) pp. 183-184. (Used by permission from Peale Center for Christian Living.)

31   In Charles Dickens, *Christmas Books* (London: OUP, 1954) pp. 13-14.

32   Quoted in Carl Ackerman, *George Eastman* (Boston: A.M. Kelly, 1930 ; reprinted., Clifton, New Jersey, 1973) p. 382.

33   Quoted in Edward Kilman and Theon Wright, *Hugh Roy Cullen: A Story of American Opportunity* (New York: Prentice Hall, 1954) p. 227.

34   Charles Dickens, *op. cit.,* pp. 74-76.

35   Andrew Carnegie, "Wealth," *North American Review,* p. 659.

36   Frederic Cople Jaher, *op. cit.,* p. 204.

37   Quoted by Jaher, *op. cit.,* p. 204.

38   W.D. Rubinstein, in W.D. Rubinstein (ed.), *Wealth and the Wealthy in the Modern World* (New York: St.Martin's Press, 1980) p. 27.

39   Carnegie, "Wealth," *North American Review,* p. 659.

40   Ibid, p. 659.

41   See "Retiree gives $36 million for scholarship funding" in *New York Times,* October 28, 1991, p. 28.

42   See Emrys Hughes (ed), *Keir Hardie's Speeches and Writings (From 1888 to 1915)* (Glasgow: "Forward" Printing and Publishing, n.d.) pp. 45-46.

43   But note that Hardie did not make the mistake of idealizing the poor: "Selfishness is not by any means a monopoly of the rich. . . .If it were possible for the ownership of land and capital to be transferred from the rich to the poor tomorrow, but in such a way that each trade would have an interest in oppressing every other, the change would be for the worse rather than for the better." See Emrys Hughes (ed), *op. cit.,* pp. 119-120.

INDEX

HAGGAI INSTITUTE

Billions of people live in nations where evangelism by outsiders is discouraged or openly prohibited. Haggai Institute selects Christians of *proven* influence from within these nations; equips them to reach their *own* people for Christ; and enables them to *reproduce* their training in others.

To achieve this, Haggai Institute utilizes two strategically located centers in Singapore and Maui and a top-grade faculty drawn almost exclusively from the non-Western world. Its program provides in-depth small-group lectures and workshops on the "how" of evangelism. It also provides unique consultative resources through which participating leaders draw up their own individual strategies for evangelism.

Since 1969, more than 19,000 Christian leaders have graduated from Haggai Institute's international and regional seminars. These men and women represent almost all denominations and vocations, and 138 countries across Asia, Africa, and Central and South America. Each is engaged in active personal evangelism, and on average will pass the training on to 100 other leaders.

For more information on the Haggai Institute ministry of world evangelism, write to: P.O. Box 13; Atlanta, Georgia 30370, U.S.A.

ABOUT THE AUTHOR

John Edmund Haggai has spent a lifetime studying and teaching leadership.

As Founder and President of Haggai Institute, he travels over 200,000 miles every year and has circled the globe more than 75 times. He can count among his friends many of the world's most distinguished and illustrious leaders.

He is a prolific writer. His first book, *How to Win Over Worry*, has been a bestseller since 1959 and is now published in over 15 languages. Among his other books are: *How to Win Over Pain, The Leading Edge, Lead On!, My Son Johnny,* and *Be Careful What You Call Impossible.*

With a reputation as an informative and captivating speaker, Dr. Haggai is sought after by international investment bankers on Wall Street and by graduate students at Yale. His audiences have included the world's largest Rotary Club; the Kiwanis International Convention; the Institute for Human Development in Seoul, Korea; and numerous civic clubs and universities across six continents.

A personal friend of Paul J. Meyer, Dr. Haggai was born in Louisville, Kentucky, and lives in Atlanta, Georgia. But his heart is in the Third World, and his vision embraces leadership and evangelism in every nation on earth.